Moodle 3.x Teaching Techniques

Third Edition

Creative ways to build powerful and effective online courses with Moodle 3.0

Susan Smith Nash

BIRMINGHAM - MUMBAI

Moodle 3.x Teaching Techniques

Third Edition

First published: September 2007

Second edition: January 2010

Third edition: May 2016

Production reference: 1200516

Published by Packt Publishing Ltd.

Livery Place

35 Livery Street

Birmingham B3 2PB, UK.

ISBN 978-1-78646-229-9

www.packtpub.com

Credits

Author

Susan Smith Nash

Commissioning Editor

Wilson D'souza

Acquisition Editor

Larissa Pinto

Content Development Editor

Anish Dhurat

Technical Editor

Murtaza Tinwala

Copy Editor

Charlotte Carneiro

Project Coordinator

Bijal Patel

Proofreader

Safis Editing

Indexer

Monica Ajmera Mehta

Production Coordinator

Manu Joseph

Cover Work

Manu Joseph

About the Author

Susan Smith Nash has been designing and developing online courses and programs for more than 15 years for education, training, and personal development.

In addition to Moodle 3.x Teaching Techniques, she is the author of a number of Moodle books and training videos, including *Moodle Course Design Best Practices* and *Moodle for Training and Professional Development*. She has also authored *Video-Assisted Mobile Learning for Writing Courses*.

I would like to thank my online students and a very special thanks and appreciation to Lic. Miguel Hermosillo and Dr. Jeff Kissinger, director of the Rollins College, Instructional Design Certificate Program.

www.PacktPub.com

eBooks, discount offers, and more

Did you know that Packt offers eBook versions of every book published, with PDF and ePub files available? You can upgrade to the eBook version at www.PacktPub.com and as a print book customer, you are entitled to a discount on the eBook copy. Get in touch with us at customercare@packtpub.com for more details.

At www.PacktPub.com, you can also read a collection of free technical articles, sign up for a range of free newsletters and receive exclusive discounts and offers on Packt books and eBooks.

https://www2.packtpub.com/books/subscription/packtlib

Do you need instant solutions to your IT questions? PacktLib is Packt's online digital book library. Here, you can search, access, and read Packt's entire library of books.

Why subscribe?

- Fully searchable across every book published by Packt
- Copy and paste, print, and bookmark content
- On demand and accessible via a web browser

Table of Contents

Preface

Welcome to *Moodle 3.x Teaching Techniques!* I am delighted to have this opportunity to work with you and help you unlock new potential using the world's most popular online learning management system program, Moodle. It has been a favorite of many of the world's most distinguished and forward-looking online programs, and now that Moodle accommodates mobile learning, as well as social media, while maintaining its intuitive, easy-to-use and easy-to-manage interface, it is appealing to students who approach the course from a wide range of devices. In addition to its convenience and ease of implementation, Moodle's cloud-based interface, Moodle has developed a solution for small users.

Moodle Cloud (`https://moodle.com/cloud/`) offers small users the ability to use Moodle via Moodle Cloud for free. You have webspace and up to 50 users, along with 200 MB storage space provided for free. It is a great opportunity for instructors, students, and administrators to create an exemplary course, which satisfies users on many different levels.

What this book covers

Chapter 1, *Developing an Effective Online Course*, covers how Moodle has kept up with best practices in online course development. Topics include the Moodle advantage, Moodle in a mobile world, instructional principles and activities, Bloom's taxonomy, and Universal Design. You will learn how to determine course objectives, write learning outcomes that align with Bloom's taxonomy, and map out an assessment strategy.

Chapter 2, *Instructional Material*, talks about how to create effective instructional material and how to organize it. Topics include selecting and organizing instructional material, guiding and motivating students, and incorporating social media and cloud-based resources. You will learn how to select materials, organize them, set up a discussion, and incorporate video, audio, and images from cloud-based sources or social media.

Chapter 3, *Collaborative Activities*, deals with the different types of forums and how best to set them up and use them. Topics include a discussion of productive online interaction, types of interaction, tying collaborative activities to learning outcomes, common pitfalls, and chat. You will learn how to set up Forums for discussions, select the right kinds of forums, and set up forums for different purposes.

Chapter 4, *Assessment*, talks about how to create different types of assessments and to match them with learning outcomes. Topics include the purpose of assessment, as it relates to learning objectives, motivation, and the automatic generation of badges and certificates.

You will learn how to develop assessments and an assessment strategy, and you will also learn how to created automatically generated certificates and badges.

Chapter 5, *Lesson Solutions*, covers developing and sequencing content for lessons, and building lessons step by step. Topics include building lessons step-by-step, selecting the elements, and controlling the flow through a lesson. Students will learn how to build a lesson and to sequence it for ideal performance. They will also learn how to develop a lesson and then how to control flow through it.

Chapter 6, *Wiki Solutions*, deals with how to create different types of wikis and how and why to use them. Topics include using a wiki to achieve learning objectives, and using social media and cloud resources. You will learn how to build different types of wikis and control student input.

Chapter 7, *Glossary Solutions*, talks about creating glossaries for activities, collaborative interaction, and assessments. Topics include helping students learn via schema building, glossaries and learning objectives, and the functions of the glossary. You will learn to build a glossary and to use it to create test questions, technical terms, and a class directory.

Chapter 8, *The Choice Activity*, deal with using the Choice activity to create polls and quizzes to engage students. Topics include polls, learning styles, using a quiz. You will learn how to create quizzes and polls.

Chapter 9, *Course Solutions*, covers creating a template for a full course. Topics include creating a course template and a course design document, and then prioritizing and selecting based on learning objectives. You will learn how to map out the steps to build a course from start to finish, create a syllabus, engagers, quizzes, assessment, and develop automatically generated certificates and badges.

Chapter 10, *Workshop Solutions*, talks about creating a workshop to encourage collaborative development of material and to use peer review to learn from each other. Topics include workshops and collaborative learning, creating the workshop that allows peer assessment. You will learn how to build a workshop and to create examples.

Chapter 11, *Portfolio/Gallery Solutions*, covers the design and development of portfolios which encourage engagement and collaboration, with results displayed in a gallery in Moodle. Topics include the advantages of collaborative activities, the design of project-based assessment, the benefits of creative capstones, the analysis of an example ("Our Hometowns"), and tips for success. You will learn how to build an effective portfolio assignment, create examples/sample portfolios, and build a gallery of examples.

What you need for this book

Make sure that you have Moodle 3.0 or later, and a good Internet connection.

Who this book is for

This book is intended for instructional designers, teachers, teaching assistants, Moodle administrators, program administrators, and instructional technologists who have an interest in highly effective, high-quality online courses, and in learning how to most effectively deploy a Moodle solution.

Conventions

In this book, you will find a number of text styles that distinguish between different kinds of information. Here are some examples of these styles and an explanation of their meaning.

Code words in text, database table names, folder names, filenames, file extensions, pathnames, dummy URLs, user input, and Twitter handles are shown as follows: "You can name it `Ancient Humanities`."

New terms and **important words** are shown in bold. Words that you see on the screen, for example, in menus or dialog boxes, appear in the text like this: "Click **Add an activity or resource** and then **Add a Forum**."

Warnings or important notes appear in a box like this.

Tips and tricks appear like this.

Reader feedback

Feedback from our readers is always welcome. Let us know what you think about this book—what you liked or disliked. Reader feedback is important for us as it helps us develop titles that you will really get the most out of.

To send us general feedback, simply e-mail feedback@packtpub.com, and mention the book's title in the subject of your message.

If there is a topic that you have expertise in and you are interested in either writing or contributing to a book, see our author guide at www.packtpub.com/authors.

Customer support

Now that you are the proud owner of a Packt book, we have a number of things to help you to get the most from your purchase.

Downloading the color images of this book

We also provide you with a PDF file that has color images of the screenshots/diagrams used in this book. The color images will help you better understand the changes in the output. You can download this file from https://www.packtpub.com/sites/default/files/downloads/Moodle3xTeachingTechniques_ColoredImages.pdf.

Errata

Although we have taken every care to ensure the accuracy of our content, mistakes do happen. If you find a mistake in one of our books—maybe a mistake in the text or the code—we would be grateful if you could report this to us. By doing so, you can save other readers from frustration and help us improve subsequent versions of this book. If you find any errata, please report them by visiting http://www.packtpub.com/submit-errata, selecting your book, clicking on the **Errata Submission Form** link, and entering the details of your errata. Once your errata are verified, your submission will be accepted and the errata will be uploaded to our website or added to any list of existing errata under the Errata section of that title.

To view the previously submitted errata, go to https://www.packtpub.com/books/content/support and enter the name of the book in the search field. The required information will appear under the **Errata** section.

Piracy

Piracy of copyrighted material on the Internet is an ongoing problem across all media. At Packt, we take the protection of our copyright and licenses very seriously. If you come across any illegal copies of our works in any form on the Internet, please provide us with the location address or website name immediately so that we can pursue a remedy.

Please contact us at `copyright@packtpub.com` with a link to the suspected pirated material.

We appreciate your help in protecting our authors and our ability to bring you valuable content.

Questions

If you have a problem with any aspect of this book, you can contact us at `questions@packtpub.com`, and we will do our best to address the problem.

1
Developing an Effective Online Course

Welcome to *Moodle 3.x Teaching Techniques*! Moodle offers teachers and course designers a toolbox full of online teaching tools. This book shows you how to use those tools to create effective learning solutions. These learning solutions are based on proven, accepted instructional principles and best practices for online courses and traditional classroom activities.

Moodle is a **Course Management System(CMS)** that is used to produce web-based courses. It is a **Free and Open Source Software (FOSS)**, which means that you are free to use, modify, and redistribute it as long as you:

- Provide the source to others
- Do not modify or remove the original license and copyrights
- Apply this same license to any derivative work

Under these conditions, thousands of developers have contributed features and functionality to Moodle. The result is the world's most popular, free, and feature-packed course management system, which is also an online learning system. Its flexibility makes it ideal for learning that is delivered by many different organizations, including schools, colleges, universities, corporate and association training, and professional development.

The Moodle advantage

Many of the features in Moodle are carefully chosen to support a philosophy of learning called **social constructionist pedagogy**. Simply stated, this style of learning and teaching is based on four concepts: constructivism, constructionism, social constructivism, and connected and separate:

- Students acquire new knowledge as they interact with their environment, your course activities, and other students.
- Students learn more when they construct learning experiences for others. You might be familiar with the process of learning described by Jerome Bruner in his *Learning Pyramid*. It states that students remember 10% of what they read, 20% of what they hear, 30% of what is demonstrated to them, 50% of what they discuss, and 75% of what they practice. This pyramid states that students retain 90% of what they teach others. You can check the learning pyramid at `http://h` `omepages.gold.ac.uk/polovina/learnpyramid`.
- When students become part of a culture, they are constantly learning. For example, you and your partner would probably learn more about ballroom dancing when you're in a dance class versus watching a video together. The interaction with other students, and possibly a variety of teachers, would enrich and accelerate your learning process.
- Some students try to remain objective and factual, some try to accept more subjective views, and others try to integrate both approaches. Constructed behavior is when a student can choose whichever approach is more appropriate.

You are probably not accustomed to an application's features being chosen based on a philosophy. Usually, features are chosen based only on what is technically feasible and what customers are willing to pay for. These are certainly factors to consider for Moodle developers. However, the educational philosophy behind Moodle is also a criterion for adding features. This gives Moodle a tremendous advantage.

As Moodle is designed around a well-defined educational philosophy, its user interface is very consistent. I don't just mean in the traditional sense, where you compare icons, colors, menu actions, and layouts on each page to ensure that they match, but as you go through a Moodle site, things look, feel, and function consistently. More importantly, you interact with each activity, your classmates, and the teacher in a consistent way, whether it's in a chat room, forum, or by leaving feedback for a workshop. When interaction becomes easier, a student can focus more on learning and less on the software.

Further, Moodle's interactive activities and features allow developers to create courses that are self-guided and self-paced and can be utilized with mobile devices as well as desktop computers.

What will we accomplish with this book

As teachers begin to use an online learning system, the first thing most of us do is explore the system's features. We discover it has online forums, electronic flashcards, interactive quizzes, Wikis, collaborative workshops, and other features. Our question now becomes, *How can I use this feature to teach my course?* or *What features of this software can be used to effectively to teach my course?* For example, we discover that the software has an `Assignment` module and ask, *How can I use online assignments in my course?* We start by exploring the software and figuring out how we can use it to effectively teach our courses. When given a new tool, it's natural to explore the tool's functions and think of ways to use it.

This book gives you solutions that help you make the most of the many features found in a standard Moodle installation. Some of these solutions require several hours to build, while others are just a matter of selecting a single option in one of Moodle's setup pages.

Effective learning and teaching principles are not just for academic teachers. If you're a corporate trainer, your students will benefit from the learning solutions in this book. These solutions are based on instructional practices that have been proven to work for young and adult learners.

Some Moodle requisites

You don't need to be an expert Moodle teacher or course creator to use the solutions in this book. However, this book assumes that you can use Moodle's basic features. You can learn Moodle before reading this book or learn it as you practice implementing these solutions.

For example, one of the learning solutions in this book is *Group Project*. This solution uses Moodle's standard wiki module. To implement the solution, you should know how to create a wiki in Moodle. You could learn how to create a wiki from another book on basic Moodle usage, online help, or from the `https://moodle.org/` forums. However, this book will not give step-by-step directions to create a wiki. It will give you directions to adapt the wiki for Group Project.

If you're new to Moodle, consider practicing on the Moodle demonstration site at `https://moodle.org/demo/`.

If you need more information about any of the features of Moodle, Moodle provides updated documentation at moodledoc. For Moodle 3.0, the moodledocs site can be found at `https://docs.moodle.org/30/en/Main_page`.

Standard modules

Moodle is an open source software, so new modules are constantly being developed and contributed by the Moodle community. The modules that are a part of Moodle's core distribution are covered in this book. Moodle's capabilities are enhanced by additional modules, which enable better learning solutions.

Some of the techniques in this book are workarounds that can be directly accomplished by adding a third-party module to your Moodle site. However, as each new version of Moodle is released, only the standard modules are guaranteed to be compatible. There is no guarantee that a third-party module that you have installed will be compatible with future versions of Moodle. This can hold back the upgrade process for your site.

All of the solutions in this book can be implemented with Moodle's standard modules. I encourage you to explore the add-on modules available at `https://moodle.org/`.

Instructional principles and activities

The solutions in this book are based on accepted, research-based instructional principles and traditional learning activities. Learning principles can be applied to a wide variety of activities. For example, the principles of Distributed Practice and Immediate Error Correction can be applied to Quiz, Lesson, and Assignment activities in Moodle. When we go through the solutions for quizzes, lessons, and assignments, we will briefly discuss how to apply these learning principles to those activities.

What are we trying to do in an online course?

In order to make the most of Moodle, it's useful to look at our overall instructional strategy. It's easy to get very excited about all the tools and activities that Moodle offers and then try to incorporate all of them. How do you decide which activities to use and how to organize the course?

The best approach is to start with your overall learning objectives. Ask a few simple questions: what do you want students to be able to do at the end of the course? How and what is the best way for them to demonstrate what they've learned in a way that is measurable?

As you answer the questions, identify five or six of your most important learning outcomes. Those will be your learning objectives.

For example, if you are teaching a course in Introduction to Geology, one of the outcomes might be for students to be able to identify three major rock types. As you state this objective, you can start thinking about how you'll have them demonstrate the fact that they can identify these major rock types. Thinking ahead to Moodle, you might have them take a quiz that requires them to recognize rock types. Or, you may ask them to post photos from their field trips with descriptive labels.

You'll find that, in Moodle, learning objectives (LOs for short) will soon become your best friends. They will help you determine how to organize the course, select course content, and create assessments.

Here are a few key points in developing learning objectives:

- Make sure that you do not have too many learning objectives. Limit them to five or six. Too many learning objectives will result in repetition and a muddy focus.
- Use active verbs that lead to measurable outcomes. One of the most important elements of course design is developing activities and instructional content that enable students to engage in tasks that can be assessed in a measurable way. Thus, it's good to avoid such fuzzy phrases such as "understand a concept" or "believe in a concept." Instead, verbs should be active with measurable outcomes. Examples of these are "describe", "list", or "create."
- Use Bloom's Taxonomy to help develop your learning objectives. Bloom's Taxonomy is a framework that was first developed in 1956 by Benjamin Bloom and other collaborators, who sought to develop categories of learning levels. Their goal was to help teachers and instructional designers plan and develop appropriate instructions, design-appropriate assessments, and align instructions and assessments with learning objectives. They did so by identifying six cognitive processes, from the most basic (on the base of a triangle) to the most complex. There are six categories (in the 2001 update), each with associated action verbs, which help teachers and designers organize instructions, from the most basic to most complex, and design effective assessments.

Here is a diagram that shows levels and then includes cognitive processes. It also includes basic verbs that you can use in designing and developing your course. You can also refer to `https://cft.vanderbilt.edu/guides-sub-pages/blooms-taxonomy/#why` for more information.

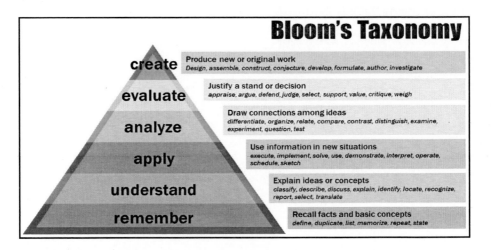

As you progress through this book, you'll find that we'll be using Bloom's Taxonomy and learning objectives to make sure that we're selecting the right materials, putting them in the right places, and also developing the right kind of assessment strategy.

How does learning take place in an online course?

If you are new to e-learning, you might think of an online course as something that involves a great deal of reading and perhaps a certain number of videos in which you watch a professor delivering a lecture to a group in a traditional classroom as he/she writes something that you can't quite see on a dusty chalkboard. The dominant mode in such a setting is passive and the very idea of this experience may give you a bit of a sinking feeling. How can you learn if you're falling asleep?

Well, the good news is that you're likely to be kept wide awake in e-learning courses, both online and mobile. You're going to be engaged and active in ways that you may never have expected from an educational setting. All the things you love about learning, connectivity, social networking, and Web 2.0 applications can be found in a well-designed course that uses Moodle as its learning management system.

A course that has been built in Moodle encourages learners to engage with the material on many different levels. Learning takes place in many ways and in different places and, above all, there is a built-in flexibility that allows the learner to approach material in ways that work for them.

Keep in mind that each learner has his/her own style and the best learning programs accommodate learning styles and preferences. So, whether or not the participants in the course are auditory, visual, or kinesthetic learners, they must be taken into consideration, and the instructional activities and assessments should reflect those possibilities. Learners should have options, not just with regard to course content but also in the approach they take to the material and to their peers.

Once the decision has been made to employ an instructional strategy that accommodates multiple learning styles and preferences, then it is possible to move forward to the next couple of steps.

How people learn

Cognitive psychologists have researched how people learn and, in doing so, have developed a wide array of models that provide explanations of how people learn. They have mapped the processes in ways that can be utilized to create effective learning experiences in both formal and informal settings.

Categories, classifications, and schemata

One of the most fundamental ways in which people learn is by creating mental file cabinets, which cognitive psychologists call *schema* or *schemata*. The approach is not new-you may be familiar with Aristotle's development of categories and, later, the classification system that the botanist Linnaeus developed. British cognitive psychologist, Frederic Bartlett, applied the concept of creating categories to learning activities and his work was further developed in the 1970s by Richard Anderson. Categories and classifications help people file, sort, retrieve, and talk about things and concepts. The development of schemata is automatic and people create categories without realizing it.

Not only do the schemas work effectively in keeping items well organized, they can help people learn to make connections across categories and compare and contrast the items.

Further, as learners begin to identify, discuss, and evaluate the items, they also practice taking the items in and out of working memory and thus the approach of classification helps in developing memory and knowledge retrieval skills as well.

Social learning

According to many psychologists, our culture shapes us and we learn from the environment and each other. According to the Russian theorist, Vygotsky, who developed his theories in the 1920s while working with school children in group settings, knowledge is transmitted (or created) by culture and groups. This may seem obvious, but the implications are rather dramatic, particularly in the case of e-learning. The group establishes what is knowledge and, by the same token, also determines what is not considered knowledge at all. An excellent example of social learning in the e-learning space is a wiki.

Of course, the major wiki that people are most familiar with is Wikipedia, the online collaborative encyclopedia. Think of how numerous authors contribute to a single Wikipedia piece and the same who contribute can also delete or challenge an item. The group decides what is knowledge and, perhaps more importantly, what is not. The Wikipedia item is always in flux and ideas about what a thing is or is not are subject to constant discussions, debates, negotiations, and mediations. The socialization process that occurs in the discussions is also a part of the social learning equation. If you don't post on Wikipedia in the correct manner, you will quickly be informed of the correct rules and approaches.

Vygotsky points out that people who fail to accept the process quickly find themselves outside the group. They may seek their own group of like-minded people. But, even in this case, knowledge is constantly in flux and people gain knowledge and learn acceptable behavior from the group.

Emulatory learning

We learn from each other and our leaders. We watch and copy what we observe. You may wonder how this is different from social learning and, certainly, there are areas of overlap. However, the idea of emulatory learning is much more basic-we see, we imitate; we hear and we echo.

You may be familiar with the *Bobo Doll* experiments of the early 1960s. In this experiment, Canadian psychologist, Albert Bandura, asked a teacher to hit a life-sized clown-shaped blow-up doll named Bobo. The teacher was filmed as she hit the Bobo doll with a stick.

Later, children around the age of five were required to watch the film of the teacher hitting the Bobo doll with a stick. Then, each child was put in a room alone with only a Bobo doll and a stick for company. Researchers observed the children's behavior behind a one-way mirror and they also filmed what transpired. What they found was that the children invariably picked up the stick and then used it to hit the Bobo doll. The interesting point is that the children seemed to enjoy the experience, which is illuminating and disturbing at the same time. The children imitated what they saw and they did it with relish.

Lesson learned? Be careful about the behavior that you are unconsciously modeling. Someone will learn from you. They will imitate you, which is either a very good thing or potentially harmful. In the e-learning space, it's an invaluable thing to keep in mind as you model positive behavior, which will then be imitated.

At the same time, knowing that people will imitate what they perceive an authority figure to be doing can help you develop examples and also recognize and reward the behaviors that you'd like others to emulate.

Making sure that the courses include a good guide and a model to follow is important. Not only will learners imitate the behaviors, they will start to feel comfortable with the processes. In the e-learning world, Bandura's notion of emulatory behavior is a cornerstone to learning in Moodle, which contains a high level of interactivity.

Communities of practice

People who share interests and skills like to work together. They share similar interests and have a strong sense of affiliation, which is often based on trust and a firm sense of mutual comprehension and acceptance.

Communities of common interests are sheltering, nurturing, and liberating. They allow freedom of expression, which is simply not possible in the world at large. People (and learners) thrive when they can work in a friendly, non-judgmental environment. This is almost axiomatic with e-learners and at-risk populations (which often comprise a large segment of the online learning community).

Communities of interest that arise from shared prior knowledge, commonly held beliefs and cultural values, and shared experiences are often powerful because they motivate learners to stay as a part of the group. They provide a strong sense of affiliation. An e-learning program that builds communities of interest around cohorts can achieve great success.

Some of the new plug-ins available for Moodle encourage the building of communities by holding synchronous *live* webinars, which can be archived and viewed later. An example is

BigBlueButton, which has been adapted for use in Moodle and can be used to keep people with similar interests in touch with each other for not just the duration of the course but on an ongoing basis, depending on the access provided.

Social practices

You've probably heard the term *learning by doing* many times but have not really considered how it relates to e-learning. The key is application. Applying the concepts by doing activities is one way of keeping the learning experience from becoming passive. In an ideal e-learning environment, application of concepts would occur often and big chunks of content are broken down into small chunks, which are then to be followed by exercises and activities. Many effective practices involve collaborative activities that encourage learners to share and build on prior knowledge.

With today's emphasis on mobile computing and the increasing ability to connect to high-speed networks, many learners want to be able to connect from any place and at any time, and, more importantly, to be able to collaborate. Further, they are accustomed to working with social media platforms such as Twitter, Facebook, LinkedIn, WhatsApp, Instagram, YouTube, and more. They are used to using social media for the purpose of obtaining and transmitting information as well as ideas. This is a breakthrough for social learning because it means that the primary philosophy of Moodle, which has social constructionism as its core, has received a big vote of confidence by the learner populace.

It is good to keep in mind that Moodle has evolved with the times and accommodates mobile devices with its "responsive" themes, which means that a device is automatically detected and Moodle's appearance will be adjusted accordingly. So, if you choose a "responsive" theme, you can expect it to have functionality and an appealing appearance on tablets, desktops, and mobile devices, such as smartphones.

Experiential learning

People sometimes wonder if the virtual world has any connection at all to the experiential world-the world of phenomena. It is easy to argue that there is no connection at all between virtual and real, particularly if it's a matter of role-playing in simulations that are not grounded in a corresponding real-life scenario.

However, when serious games, simulations, role-playing, and other virtual world activities have a corresponding counterpart in the real world, then it is possible to have experiential learning. Further, experiential learning that has taken place in the real world and is then reinforced by role-playing, simulations, or serious games, can be highly effective.

Experiential learning in Moodle can take place in a traditional e-learning space and it can also occur in a mobile learning environment. When the content of a course is related to what one has learned previously or involves actual field work, data collection, and peer interaction via a mobile device, the experience can be quite powerful. For example, a course on environmental management could incorporate the use of mobile devices in conjunction with GPS. The GIS information could be collected, photos taken and tagged according to latitude, longitude, and time/date, and then the details could be shared with group members. The concepts, practical application, and social reinforcement would take place in a single learning event.

Another possible way to share experiential learning would be to post videos to share and then post "response" videos. A variety of "conversations" can ensue crosses disciplines and learning modalities and these can enable students to feel like they are working with a live document and dynamic process, rather than the static experience that characterizes much of traditional learning.

Moodle's learning environment incorporates the practices of social media, which makes it comfortable for individuals who are used to using apps on their smartphones, tablets, and computers to incorporate Moodle's similar functions.

Further, depending on the level of access at the institution, the administrator may also enable the use of social media sites such as Facebook and Twitter. Plus, it is easy to embed html code in order to provide instant access to videos on sites such as YouTube, audio on SoundCloud, or images on sites such as Flickr.

Conditions of learning

In order for the mind to be receptive to new ideas and start the learning process, it is necessary to capture the learner's interest. Gagne and other researchers investigated the problem of getting learning started and they found that, unless certain "conditions of learning" were met, it would be very difficult to assure that learning takes place. One of the most important elements was to have an engaging experience. There must be spillover from the affective domain to the cognitive domain. In other words, learners must feel emotionally engaged in order to have ideal learning conditions.

In an e-learning course, there are several ways to create conditions of learning. One can engage the learner by making them feel curious, puzzled, or emotionally connected to the course content. You can relate the content to their lives and current controversies or contemporary issues. You can use sound, color, design, and animations to keep the course lively (without being too distracting).

One good way to start a course or unit is to kick it off with an illustrative scene or a case study that resonates with the learner's own experience of life. One might use the strategy of **in medias res**—jumping in the middle of things—for an emotional appeal. Remember that you're using a sound rhetorical strategy-one that Aristotle referred to as "pathos", and this is one of the most effective strategies in order to gain and keep the attention of others.

Cognitive psychologists have also looked at the importance of readying the brain to learn by having learners engage in "brain warm-ups". These typically consist of questions that trigger the desire to learn by sparking interest and triggering curiosity. Moodle's activities, such as **Choice**, can be set up to create little **did you know** introductory interactive experiences that use not just text but also graphics.

 Not only do the "brain warm-ups" help trigger interest, they also motivate the learner and thus build in mechanisms that are designed to help students successfully complete their course.

Behaviorism

Operant conditioning has a place in e-learning. We're not really talking about conditioning as basic as Pavlov's dog, but it is important to keep in mind that positive reinforcement works wonders in e-learning.

There are several ways to build positive responses to desirable behaviors. For example, feedback from the instructor can be timely and always start with a positive note. Students can be guided to provide positive responses in collaborative work. In the case of automated activities, responses can be built and information is provided in a positive way.

Recent versions of Moodle, including Moodle 3.0, accommodate exciting new plugins that reward the successful completion of both small chunks of learning as well as completion of the entire unit or course. Badges can be displayed not just in the course but also on one's personal website or social media site, such as Facebook or LinkedIn. For example, Moodle works well with Mozilla's Open Badge program, which can be found at `http://openbadg es.org/`.

In addition to this, Moodle can be set to automatically generate certificates of successful completion after completing all the activities in a unit plus achieving a passing score (which is set by the administrator). Seeing the fruits of one's labor, especially when it can be used to advance one's career, academic, and personal aspirations and goals, can be a powerful way to reward actions, reinforce positive behaviors, and motivate learners.

Course-building components in Moodle

As you start building your course in Moodle, you'll have a number of components to choose from. As in the case of all formal learning programs, it is important to start by identifying course outcomes and learning objectives.

After you have finished learning objectives and course outcomes, you will develop a plan to build your course, which maps the Moodle components (resources and activities) to your learning objectives. How to create effective course outcomes and learning objectives will be dealt with in a future chapter. At this point, we'll simply list the materials you have to work with in Moodle. You will come to appreciate and enjoy the variety and flexibility.

Resources

As you build your course, you may wish to start clustering your readings, links to outside resources, and media. The Resources group, with all the tools associated with it, will help you do so. We are not going to go over every resource tool in Moodle. We'll just start with the most popular ones. We will discuss more complex tools in future chapters and sections.

Book

The Book toolallows you to create a collection of digital assets that you can bundle together in order to create the instructional content for your course. In Moodle, a *Book* is not an e-book, a PDF, or any other kind of rigid content item. Instead, it is a dynamic collection of digital objects that come together as a kind of repository for learners.

The *Book* is generally a collection of web pages and so what students will see is a set of links, usually with descriptions and perhaps brief instructions. This repository constitutes the core knowledge base in your course and from it, learners should be able to define, describe, list, and recognize key concepts.

Link to a file or website

Perhaps the most used instructional content tool besides the Book tool is the link to a file or website tool. This tool allows you to create a link to outside web-based resources and incorporate a description and guiding materials.

It is useful to point out that it is possible to incorporate html and embed a resource as well. Embedding is particularly useful for graphics, video, and audio resources because it makes it possible to play media resources from within Moodle without having to leave the site and to go another site. Further, embedded media sites are often sized so that they fit well on a page and one can conveniently stop and restart the media.

Activities

Many instructors like to organize their course chronologically, not only because it is practical, but also because the tools lend themselves to the sequential presentation of material. Once they have their basic structure in place, they then add Resources and Activities.

Many Moodle users like to build their courses on a foundation of Forums and then, when they feel more comfortable, they take advantage of the more complex resources such as Books, Assignments, Choices, and more. Keep in mind that, in Moodle, the resources are added by using the tool of the same name. So, if you want to add a Forum, you would need to use the Forum tool. This section lists many of the popular Activity tools and provides a brief overview of each to give you an idea of how to use them.

Assignment

The Assignment tool is where the instructor defines a task that the learner must complete. It often links back to study materials (which have been created in using the Book tool).

Choice

The Choice toolallows you to create multiple choice questions. They can be used in both reviews and assessments. They can also be used to create polls and questionnaires for students to indicate interest and for the instructor to find out important things about their group.

Database

The Database toolallows instructors and students to upload information. This is a great way to share resources, makes it possible to ask students to give final presentations (using presentation software), and develop engaging assignments and final projects such as student galleries and portfolios. It is also an excellent way for students to share resources and evaluate the reliability of the online sources that they have found.

Forum

The Forum tool will allow you to create dynamic and highly engaging collaborative learning activities. You can develop discussion boards, peer review areas, and also group project spaces.

Glossary

The Glossary tool is excellent for courses that require students to be able to identify and define a broad range of items and master and use a new vocabulary. If designed well, activities that employ the Glossary tool can help students develop schema-building approaches.

Quizzes

Moodle allows you to use quiz builders. Moodle 3.0 has four new quiz types, which makes the experience even more enjoyable and interactive.

Journal

The Journal toolallows students to keep learning diaries and to update journals as living documents. It also accommodates peer reviews and collaborations and can easily be incorporated into a workshop.

Lessons

The Lesson toolis an organizational tool that allows you to organize elements, list key concepts, and provide unit overviews and learning objectives.

Wiki

The Wiki toolis often used when collaboration is needed because it is a bit more flexible than the Forum tool.

Course Timetable

This tool is one of many that is excellent for assuring student success. It allows students to set deadlines, which facilitates the process of goal setting, which can be very motivating.

Instructional principles and activities mapped to Moodle features

The following table maps Moodle features to their instructional functions:

Moodle feature	Instructional function	Learning theory
Book	Knowledge base, core instructional material, content repository, and comprehension	Schemata-building
Assignment	Organization	Conditions of learning
Chat	Interactive, collaborative learning, comprehension, and evaluation	Social learning, communities of practice, and emulatory learning
Choice	Classification, application, analysis, and comprehension	Schemata
Database	Analysis and collaborative learning	Experiential learning and social practices
Moodle feature	Instructional function	Learning theory
Forum	Collaborative learning, analysis, and synthesis	Social practices, communities of practice, and experiential behaviorism
Glossary	Comprehension and schemata-building	Schemata and conditions of learning
Quiz	Comprehension and analysis	Schemata, emulatory learning, and behaviorism/operant conditioning
Wiki	Collaborative learning, application, synthesis, and evaluation	Social learning, social practice, and communities of practice
Workshop	Application and evaluation	Social practice and experiential learning
Timetable	Organization	Conditions of learning

Access for everyone

One of the concerns that learners have about e-learning is access. What if you have low-vision and limited mobility? Can Moodle work for you?

As you put together a course in Moodle, you may wish to follow design principles that assure access and are also compliant with laws designed to assure access for those with disabilities. In the United States, the **Americans with Disability Act** (**ADA**) is the law that defines the ways in which organizations need to provide access.

In order to assure compliance, the U.S. Department of Education and the **Center for Applied Special Technology** (**CAST**) collaborated in 2011 on a set of guidelines, which are known as the University Design for Learning.

There are three main categories:

- Provide Multiple Means of Representation
- Provide Multiple Means of Action and Expression
- Provide Multiple Means of Engagement

The key in UDL is to provide viable alternatives for individuals who may need accommodations. Giving options and multiple means of representation, action, expression, and engagement is possible using Moodle and this book will incorporate UDL guidelines.

For an excellent graphical representation from CAST, download the PDF file from `http://www.udlcenter.org/sites/udlcenter.org/files/updateguidelines2_0.pdf`.

Summary

This chapter presented ideas about how people learn in an online environment and it provided a brief overview of the functions and features of Moodle. Some of these features include book, chat, assignment, quiz, wiki, workshop, and more. These constitute building blocks that allow you to create unique courses that you can easily replicate thanks to the object-oriented philosophy of Moodle.

We also discussed competing theories about how people learn and why that matters to the instructor and also to the instructional designer who is building the course. The chapter also presented basic information about how Moodle is organized and what type of resources it has that can be used by instructors to build the kind of courses that they find useful. Finally, the chapter described a strategy to get started with Moodle that helps instructors develop a course, which facilitates the learning process and helps create a learning community.

2
Instructional Material

Deciding what you'll put in your course can be one of the most rewarding aspects of course development. Because Moodle has so many options, you'll enjoy flexibility and also ease of use. With Moodle, you'll be able to incorporate a wide range of instructional materials and applications, all of which can help you expand the ways in which you can engage your students and encourage them to interact with each other. You'll be able to include videos, audio files, presentations, and animations in addition to documents and graphics.

Another benefit of using Moodle is the simplicity of a forum-based structure that allows you to keep your ultimate goals in mind and to clearly match the materials with your outcomes. Once you've selected your instructional materials, Moodle makes it very easy for you to get started and create a structure that flows nicely from topic to topic and facilitates the teaching and the learning process.

This chapter offers you solutions for selecting and organizing your course materials so that you're always focused on learning objectives, course outcomes, dynamic student engagement, and strong student performance. The first section in this chapter focuses on the best ways to select and organize your course material. The later sections focuses on developing and managing a framework for your materials by employing forums.

Selecting and organizing the material

If you're like most instructors, you love your subject and the idea of sharing information gives you great satisfaction. However, you have probably noticed that it's easy to overload your students or to give them materials in a way that tends to confuse them. How can you avoid overloading and confusing your students?

One of the most effective ways to do so is to make sure that you base your selections of instructional materials on course outcomes and on the learning objectives for each unit.

Keep in mind what you'd like your students to be able to do after they complete the course. What is the basic, enduring knowledge they will take with them after the course is over? What kind of fundamental change do you want to occur in terms of the students' abilities? What kind of new skills will they be able to perform?

Once you answer these questions, you will have a list of learning outcomes. Keep them in mind as you select the instructional material you wish to use in your course.

It is often convenient to develop a map or a diagram that connects your learning outcomes with the course materials and the assessments you will use. Consider what you want your students to learn and how you'd like them to perform. Also, shape the sequence you will build and how you'll present the materials.

Matching the material to the learning objectives

As you plan your course, it is important to select your instructional material so that it aligns to the learning objectives of your course.

As you organize the material, it is often useful to arrange it so that it is increasing complexity. You may use Bloom's Taxonomy as a guide. Build on the knowledge and create effective scaffolding and make it clear how the instructional material ties to the performative aspects of the course and the assessment.

Using Forums to present your material

We'll start with an approach that is very easy to implement, which is ideal if you're just getting started and need a solution that would be good for all kinds of e-learning, including mobile learning and guided independent study.

Basically, we'll use the Forum tool to organize all the instructional content. In Moodle, the Forum is a key activities tool and you'll use it often. Later, as you feel more comfortable, you can add more tools (Book, Chat, Assignment, Choice, and so on). For now, however, we will focus on getting you operational as quickly and easily as possible.

Using the Forum activity to structure your course and to organize your content is conceptually very elegant. Students simply move from forum to forum and access the material they need. Any comments they have, assignments, or discussion items can be completed in the appropriate thread.

Plus, Moodle 3.0 has different types of forums, each with special attributes and functionality which makes it easy to deliver content in a way that aligns with your instructional strategy. The following are a few of the forums:

- The **News forum** is perfect for posting the syllabus, announcements, and key information. It is a good place for posting updates that all students need to see. One thing that is new in Moodle 3.0 is the ability for students to subscribe to updates to the News forum. The instructor can force subscription so that all the participants are automatically subscribed to the RSS feed and thus automatically receive notices. The subscription to updates in the News forum can be a real lifesaver for both instructor and student because the issues involving required performance (activities, assessment, and more) and deadlines are usually the most anxiety-producing.

- *Standard forum for general use* is the default. In this format, there is a starter post for the discussion. The instructor or the administrator starts the thread and posts the introductory words. Students may reply and may also start new threads.

- *Single, simple discussion* does not allow students to start their own threads. They can only reply to the instructor's posts. This type of forum is excellent for forums dedicated for delivering official instructional materials. Because Moodle 3.0 allows you to embed HTML code and to link to social media sites, including access portals for cloud-based repositories such as Dropbox, Box, and Google Drive, there is the added benefit, that if students encounter problems, they can mention them. The chances are, other students will have the same question or comment, so, when the instructor responds, it puts multiple learners at ease at the same time.

- The *Question and Answer forum* creates a structure that encourages meaningful interaction. Students must post a reply to the teacher's post before they can see the posts of fellow students. So it's ideal for posting responses to instructional materials and it can be tied to certain learning objectives, especially ones that involve identifying, describing, and explaining.

- The **Standard forum displayed in a blog-like format** keeps the appearance very clean because the posts are abbreviated. The oldest appears first and the others beneath it in chronological order depending on the replies.

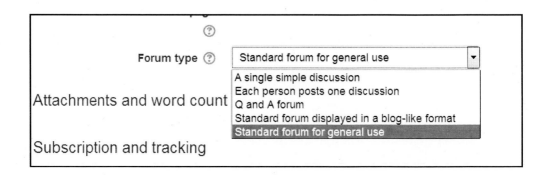

When you use the Forum activity, you will use the Moodle text editor to create messages. Keep in mind that your messages can contain text, graphics, audio, video, presentations, and more, which allows you flexibility and ease of use.

As you plan your course, it's always good to have a certain number of forums dedicated to student success and support. This is where you can post welcome messages, timelines and course calendars, lists of assignments, the syllabus, links to useful resources, and a place for students to ask questions and share their experiences. If you choose the News forum for the ones that directly relate to a student's success, you'll be assured that your students will receive key information, especially if you subscribe everyone to the forum. However, be careful to use the News forum only for the most important items. Forums that feature useful resources and possible shared activities could be placed in a question and answer forum. Student questions and comments/shared experiences can be in a standard forum.

A "key to student success" forum is one that clearly states what you hope to achieve in the course. By listing course outcomes in this forum as well as in other forums, you'll shape the students' approach to the course content and they will have a better idea of how to organize the information they will encounter.

After you've developed your **student success and support** forums, you can start creating a separate forum for each unit, which begin to identify the learning objectives, and the resources you can put in each one that go towards creating a learning environment. It is often a good idea to create a separate forum for each graded assessment. Having a separate forum for each assessment will make your job easier if you have changes to make or if you want to replace it with an assignment tool.

In fact, by populating your course with a series of separate forums, you are creating a flexible template that can be easily modified by replacing a forum with another, or with a different type of tool (Choice, Assignment, Chat, Database, Book, Journal, or more).

It is often helpful to create a course map wherein you draw all the elements you'll have in your course. List the course outcomes and then map each one to the instructional material, activities, and assessments that go with each one. This will help you as you start building your forums

Here is an example of how you can put together a course in which you organize the content around forums:

- Forum 1: Welcome, Course Overview, and Objectives
- Forum 2: Meet Your Instructor
- Forum 3: Introduce Yourself
- Forum 4: Questions for the Instructor
- Forum 5: Syllabus and Timeline
- Forum 6: Unit 1: Unit Learning Objectives
- Forum 7: Unit 1: Instructional Materials
- Forum 8: Unit 1: Discussion Questions
- Forum 9: Unit 1: Review for Quiz
- Forum 10: Unit 1: Quiz

As you can see, the structure is very straightforward and avoids the complexity of multiple tools. Keep in mind that more complex tools can always be added later to replace a forum structure. As you design your threads, consider how you will assess each one and how you'll tie it to the gradebook. You may also wish to make sure that all your students respond to the threads at more or less the same time. Moodle 3.0 allows you to set the time in which the threads can be seen by the student. You can set the time by following this sequence: **Administration** | **Site administration** | **Plugins** | **Activity modules** | **Forum.**

Incorporating social media and cloud-based resources

Start by selecting the activity tool, Forum and opening a page that requires you to indicate the settings for the forum you wish to add to. Moodle 3.0 offers many new features that facilitate the incorporation of social media and cloud-based resources.

You may embed audio and video in your Moodle course. To do so, be sure to enable the Multimedia plugins filter. Here is the sequence: **Administration** | **Site administration** | **Appearance** | **Media embedding**.

You can embed it as a file resource by uploading the file. You may also use it as a URL resource and include an icon as the display option. You may use the Moodle media button in the text editor or simply type the URL of the media file. Then the media file will automatically default to the appropriate multimedia player.

The following players can be used (be sure to use the embedded HTML provided by the host). You may need to download plugins and they need to be up-to-date:

- YouTube (hosted on YouTube)
- Vimeo (hosted on Vimeo)
- `.mp3`-MPEG audio stream
- `.flv`-flash video
- `.swf`-Macromedia Flash animation File (Adobe, Inc.)

Creating a separate group for each student

Start by selecting the activity tool, Forum and opening a page that requires you to indicate the settings for the forum you wish to add to.

First decide the place where it will be most effective. In this case, I'm placing the forum after a lesson and chat. I'm placing it there because it gives students a way to assemble materials. Click **Add an activity or resource** and then **Add a Forum**:

✛ This Is Not Your Grandmother's Beach

Edit ▾

What's new in beach communities -- how and why coastal communities have changed.

✛ ▫▫ Attracting Passionate & Quirky Affinity Groups: Edit ▾ 👤
Save the Sea Turtles, Stand-Up Paddleboarding,

ZombieNights, and more ✎

The new beach scene is all about affinity groups, who like both quirkiness and flexibility. You're likely to find sea turtle nurseries, stand-up paddleboarding (SUP), and Zombie-themed music, film, and costume-fests, all in the same community and on the same beach.

Beach tourism has evolved far, far beyond the idea of sunbathing and beach volleyball.

In this lesson, we explore some of the winners and losers in the beach community tourism game.

✛ 💬 Attracting Loyal and Passionate Tourists ✎ Edit ▾ 👤

Use this chat space to get to know each other and to discuss the projects and collaborations on how to attract affinity tourists who can be loyal and passionate.

＋ Add an activity or resource

Your forum will give you a chance to engage students so that they can share new information and insights.

The following steps illustrate how to create a separate forum for each group in your course:

1. From the **Add an activity...** drop-down list, select **Forum.**

2. Enter a **Forum name** and **Forum type** for the forum. In the following example, I'm using **A single simple discussion** to create a single-topic forum where all the postings will be displayed on the same page. This makes the history of the student-teacher discussion very easy to see. This type of forum is most useful for short, focused discussions.

3. By selecting **Yes, forever** for **Force everyone to be subscribed?** you ensure that all students are subscribed automatically, even students that enroll at a later time.

4. The key setting here is **Group mode**. When we select **Separate groups**, we create a separate forum for each group in the class. In the next section, we will create a group for each student. The result is a separate forum for each student, available only to that student and the teacher, where they can a hold private conversation.

5. Save the forum settings and continue.

Enrolling students

If you have not already enrolled students in the course, you should do so before creating the groups. If the students are already enrolled, move to *Creating a group for each student* in the next section.

The following steps illustrate how to manually enroll students in your course:

1. Open the course into which you want to enroll the students. Then, from the **Course Administration** drop-down box, select **Enrolled users**, as shown in the following screenshot:

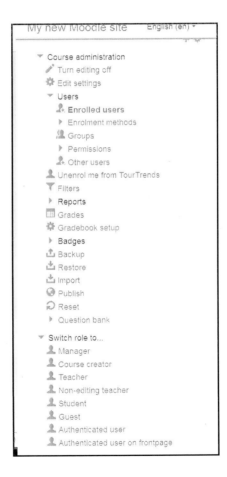

2. On the **Enrol users** page select **Student**, as shown in the following screenshot:

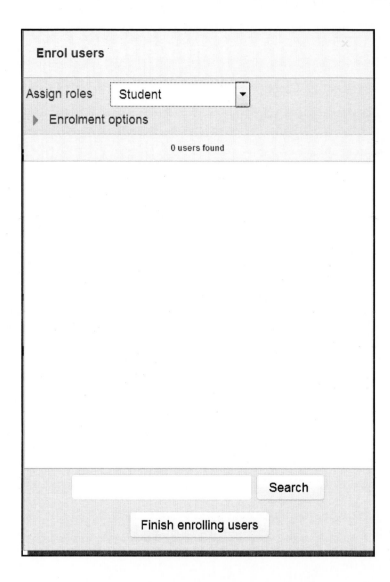

3. Ensure the **Role to assign** drop-down list is set to **Student**. Then, from the list of potential users on the right, select one user. Click the left-facing arrow to enroll that user in your course (refer to the following screenshot):

4. Repeat this for each student. If you want to remove a student from the course, select the student from the list on the left and click the right-facing arrow.

5. To exit this page, select the course name from the navigation breadcrumbs at the top of the page. This will put you back into your course's homepage and then you can continue with creating a group for each student.

Creating a group for each student

After all of your students are enrolled, go into the course and create a group for each student.

The following steps illustrate how to create groups and assign students to them:

1. From the **Course Administration** block select **Groups**, as shown in the following screenshot:

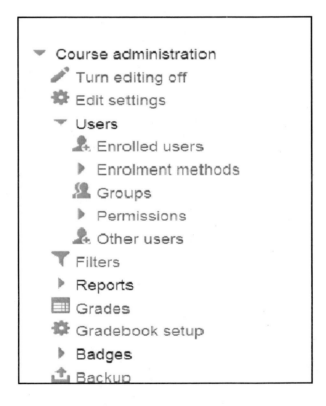

2. From the **Current role** drop-down list, select **Student**. This ensures that you are seeing only users who are enrolled as students in this course. Then, in the field above the **Add new group** button, enter the name of the first group. Name the group after the student for whom you created it. In this example, I created a group for **Moodle Student1** called **Student1** and I am about to create a group for **Moodle Student2** called **Student2**.

3. After creating all of the groups, add one student to each group. In the following

example, you can see that the group **Student1** is selected and **Moodle Student1** is a member of that group.

4. To assign a student to a group:
    1. Select the group. In the preceding example, you can see the user is about to select the group, **Student2**.
    2. Select the student to add to the group.
    3. Click the **Add selected to group** button.
    4. Repeat as needed.

5. To exit this page, select the course name from the navigation breadcrumbs at the top of the page. This will put you back into your course's homepage.

The student's private forum will look like any other Moodle forum. However, only the student and teacher will have access to it.

Guiding and motivating students

The best online courses create learning communities in which all learners have a sense that they are part of a friendly, supportive group. They eagerly post in the forums and they respond to each other quickly in a positive and productive way. They share their thoughts and impressions and you start to feel as though people are really getting to know each other. Learning is fun, even exhilarating. Some students can't wait to log on and participate.

Moodle 3.0 encourages productive interaction and collaboration and it becomes easy to share information that humanizes the learning space. For example, you can very easily use your smartphone to video a few introductory thoughts and then upload it directly to YouTube. You can then embed the post (which will include a small image/screen-capture for your video). If your videos are less than 2 minutes in length, you'll engage your students and also encourage them to share thoughts and ideas.

Creating the learning environment

There are a few tried and tested ways to optimize the interactive forum experience. Here is a brief list:

- Provide timely feedback and make sure that you maintain a positive and productive tone
- Be sure to provide positive, encouraging suggestions
- Post videos, audio files, images, and personal thoughts about that content

- Post questions that are engaging and which tie to learning objectives
- Encourage individuals to connect the course material to personal experience and then post about it
- Make participation in the forums a part of students' grades
- Model positive forum behavior by showing open-mindedness

Asking permission and setting a policy

Some activities in Moodle are almost always individual. When students complete these activities, they have a reasonable expectation that their work will not be shared with the class. For example, when a student answers a quiz question, he/she reasonably expects that what he/she wrote will not be shared with the entire class. Other activities do not carry this expectation of privacy. For example, when a student posts to a forum, he/she expects that their post will be read by the rest of the class.

Students feel good when they see their work acknowledged. They also feel confident when they know what is expected. We can use the forum to answer students' questions, but there are other ways to use the forums to acknowledge work and to help the students develop an "I can do it" attitude.

One good way is to build a forum that includes samples of successful student work. The students can see how other students-often students in the past-approached their work. They can get a good idea of how to get started and they can feel less intimidated by fear of the unknown.

Let's create a forum named **sample work**. Before posting work from a student in the sample work forum, consider if the student can reasonably expect that work to be private. If so, ask the student's permission before posting it. In any case, be sure to remove identifying names and labels. That is, remove anything from the work that would indicate which student created it. This might make the student more comfortable with having the work posted in the **sample work** forum.

If you expect to use the **sample work** forum in a class, you should clearly indicate that in the course syllabus and introduction. The idea that they have guidelines and live documents as instructional material and models can be a big relief to students. However, if any student is uncomfortable with having his/her work posted (even if it has been anonymized), please be sure to let them know you respect their wishes. The forum should be a friendly and supportive place.

Types of forums

In Moodle, you can create several types of forums. Each type can be used in a different way to get the best out of it. The types of forums are:

Types	Description
News forum	A News forum is very effective for general announcements. Each course is limited to one News forum. The News forum is automatically created for each course and appears on the front page of the Moodle site. The default settings enroll each person so that they are subscribed to the News forum.
A single simple discussion	The entire forum appears on one page. The first posting, at the top of the page, is the topic for the forum. This topic is usually created by the teacher. The students then post replies under this topic. A single-topic forum is most useful for short, highly-focused discussions.
Standard forum for general use	In a standard forum, anyone can start a new topic. Teachers and students can create new topics and reply to existing postings.
Each person posts one discussion	Each student can create one and only one new topic. Everyone can reply to every topic.
Q and A forum	This is like a single-topic forum, in that the teacher creates the topic for the forum. Students then reply to that topic. However, a student cannot see anyone else's reply until he/she has posted a reply. The topic is usually a question posed by the teacher and the students' replies are usually answers to that question. This is the standard forum in a blog-like format.

Each of these forum types can be used to create a different kind of sample work forum. The subsections coming up cover the use of each forum type.

You select the forum type while creating the forum on the **Editing Forum** page:

Single simple discussion forum

The forum consists of one topic at the top of the page and everything else on that page is a reply from the students. Readers can reply to the topic but not create new ones.

This is especially useful if you want to select the best work as an example for each topic or week in your course. You can always end each topic or week with the best work as an example so that discussion can take place around it.

Standard forum

In a standard forum, the default setting allows students to create new topics and post replies to the topics. This makes it an open forum, which would be useful if you want your students to be able to post their own work or if you want to post examples or models that you could label "sample work".

One way to keep the sample work forum organized is to allow only the teacher to create new topics. Each topic is an example of student work, posted by the teacher. Students discuss each example by replying to the topic. To accomplish this, you'll need to disable the students' ability to create new topics.

By default, the **Student** role in Moodle enables students to create new topics in a standard forum. You can disable this by referring to the following steps:

1. Select the forum in which you want to disable the students' ability to create new topics.
2. Select **Update this Forum**.
3. Review the **Forum administration | Permissions** and then customize who has the permission to modify the different categories and aspects of the **Activity: Forum**:

4. Select **Student**. This brings up the **Overrides** page.
5. For the setting **Start new discussions**, select **Prevent**.
6. Click the **Save changes** button.

In Moodle, you can administer permissions by prohibiting roles and by using the settings **Prevent** and **Allow**:

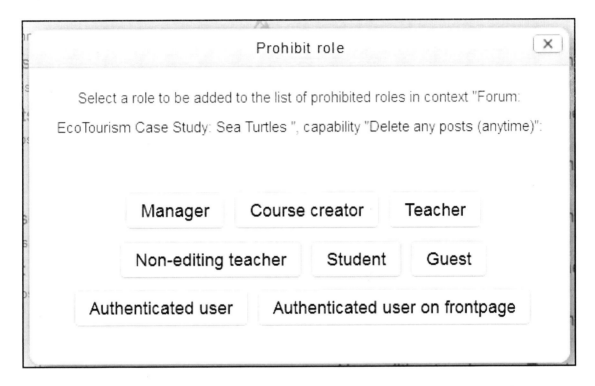

However, you could set this to **Prevent** for a specific course because a course is a lower context than the entire site; for that course, the permission **Prevent** will override the site-wide setting of **Allow**. A single activity, such as this forum, is the lowest context in Moodle. You may also choose to **Allow** roles rather than **Prevent**.

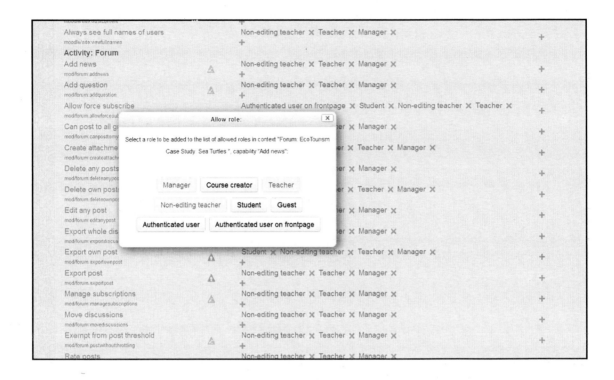

Moodle's online help has a good discussion about the differences between **Inherit**, **Allow**, **Prevent**, and **Prohibit**. It also describes how conflicts between permissions are solved by the software. If you're going to use **Override roles** elsewhere in Moodle, read this section.

Keeping discussions on track

One of the biggest challenges in using forums for an online class is keeping discussions focused on the topic. This becomes even more difficult when you allow students to create new topics in a forum. It is important to relate each topic to the learning objectives. It can be useful to refer back to the specific learning objective and even map it to the assessments. Moodle offers two tools that you can use to help keep discussions on track: custom scales and splitting discussions.

Using a custom scale to rate relevance

Moodle enables you to use a scale to rate student's work. A scale offers you something other than a grade to give the student as feedback. Scales can be used to rate forum postings, assignment submissions, and glossary entries.

To create and apply a custom scale, follow these steps:

1. Users with the roles **Administrator**, **Course creator**, and **Teacher** can create custom scales.
2. From the **Administration** block, click on **Scales**. This displays the **Scales** page.
3. On the **Scales** page, click on the **Add a new scale** button. This displays the **Editing scale** page.
4. On the **Editing scale** page:
   - Enter a **Name** for the scale. When you apply the scale to the forum, you will select the scale by this name.
   - In the **Scale** box, enter the items on your scale. Separate each item with a comma.
   - Write a **Description** for your scale. Students can see the description, so use this space to explain how they should interpret the scale.
5. Select the **Save changes** button. You are now ready to apply the scale.
6. Create or edit the forum to which you want to apply the scale. The key setting on the **Editing Forum** page is **Allow posts to be rated?**
7. When you review the student postings in the forum, you can rate each posting using the scale you created, as shown in the following screenshot:

8. When you finish rating the postings, click on the **Send in my ratings** button at the bottom of the page to save your ratings.

Splitting discussions

Users with the roles Administrator, Course creator, or Teacher can split a discussion. When you split a discussion at a post, the selected post and the ones below become a new topic.

 Note that you cannot take a few posts from the middle of a topic and split them into a new discussion. Splitting takes every post that is nested below the selected one and puts it into a new topic.

Before the split	After the split
Topic 1	New Topic 1-2
Reply 1-1	Reply 1-2-1
Reply 1-2	Reply 1-2-2
Reply 1-2-1	Reply 1-2-3
Reply 1-2-2	Topic 1
Reply 1-2-3	Reply 1-1
Reply 1-3	Reply 1-3
Reply 1-4	Reply 1-4
Reply 1-4-1	Reply 1-4-1
Reply 1-4-2	Reply 1-4-2

Will splitting move replies you want to keep in place?

In this example, the teacher was lucky. Under the pro-coup posting, there were no pro-uprising replies. If there were, those replies would have come with the pro-coup posting and the teacher would not have been able to make a topic that was completely pro-coup.

As the split function takes all of the replies nested under the split point, when a discussion has gone off course and come back on course, you should consider whether you really want to split the discussion.

Consider the following example. In **Reply 1-2**, the conversation went **off topic**. For the next two replies, it remained **off topic**. But then, **Reply 1-2-3** brought the conversation **back on topic**. Should you split the conversation at **Reply 1-2**? If you do, you'll move **Reply 1-2-3**, which is on topic, out of **Topic 1**. When it's taken out of **Topic 1**, will **Reply 1-2-3** still make sense?

Before the split	After the split

Topic 1
    Reply 1-1
    Reply 1-2 (off topic)
        Reply 1-2-1 (off topic)
        Reply 1-2-2 (off topic)
        Reply 1-2-3 (back on topic)
    Reply 1-3
    Reply 1-4
    Reply 1-4-1
    Reply 1-4-2
	Reply 1-2 (off topic)
	    Reply 1-2-1 (off topic)
	    Reply 1-2-2 (off topic)
	    Reply 1-2-3 (back on topic)
	Topic 1
	    Reply 1-1
	    Reply 1-3
	    Reply 1-4
	        Reply 1-4-1
	    Reply 1-4-2

Before splitting a forum thread, consider these two issues:

- How will rearranging the topics change the meaning of the forum?
- Will splitting move any replies that you want to keep in place?

Monitoring student participation in a forum

One of the most important tasks that you face when managing a forum is determining which students are participating and which are not. Moodle gives you several ways to get this information.

Determining who has posted to a forum

Moodle's log files can tell you who has participated in an activity. We will look at how useful log files are in determining which students have posted to a forum.

In order to view the list of students who have posted to a forum, follow these steps:

1. Enter the course for which you want the report.
2. From the **Administration** block, select **Reports**.
3. Under **Choose which logs to see**, select the settings for the following:
    - **Course**: This will be set to the course you are in, but you can choose a different course.
    - **Participants**: Leave this set to **All participants** so that you see the log for all students in the course.
    - **Dates**: To see who has ever posted to a forum, leave this set to **All**

days.

- **Activity**: In this case, it is the forum named **Using a CustomScale**.
- **Actions**: In this case, it is **Add** a posting to the forum.
- **Display**: In this case, I will display the report on screen. You can also download it as a text or Excel file.

4. Click on the **Get these logs** button. The students who have posted to the forum will be displayed.

What postings has a student made

In the preceding section, we started with the forum and displayed which students have contributed to it. You can also start with the student and see what that student has posted to any forum.

To see the postings that a student has made to all forums in a Moodle site, follow these steps:

1. Enter the course for which you want the report.
2. From the **Navigation** block, select **Participants**. A list of the students, teachers, and course creators for this course is displayed.
3. Select the student whose forum postings you want to see. The student's public profile page is displayed.
4. Select the **Forum posts** link. Under this tab, you will see two links: **Posts** and **Discussions**.
5. The **Posts** link displays all the replies the student has contributed to forums on this site. The **Discussions** link displays all the new topics (new discussions) the student has contributed to.
6. The **Activity reports** link displays all the activities the student has engaged in on the entire site. It has several links. The **Outline report** is easier to read and also shows you all the forums that the student is enrolled in and has posted to.

Summary

Forums are one of Moodle's strongest features. You can use them as building blocks in which you organize the instructional material for the entire course.

We saw how a custom scale can be used to rate the relevance of postings; you can also use custom scales to have students rate any other aspect of a forum posting. For example, suppose your class was writing a play. You could have students contribute story ideas and character sketches to a forum. Then, the class could use a custom scale to vote on whether to include them in the play.

In classes that require student participation, Moodle's log files can quantify a student's participation in class discussion. Splitting a discussion can bring it back on track when it has been taken over by an unintended subject.

Whenever you need to involve students in a discussion, a Moodle forum offers a place for students and teachers to have a productive discussion.

In the next chapter, we will continue to work with the ways in which Moodle 3.0 encourages learning through interaction and collaboration.

3
Collaborative Activities

It has often been said that the quality of an online course can be assessed through the quality of the interaction.

The fact that Moodle makes it possible to have high-quality, personalized, and very meaningful interaction means that it is possible to construct high-quality courses and to engage multiple strategies in order to achieve the desired learning outcomes. Moodle 3.0 allows a wide range of collaborative activities because it not only provides its own platform for both live (synchronous) and archived (asynchronous) collaboration, it also allows you to incorporate your existing social media chat, such as from Twitter, Skype, or BigBlueButton. It just depends on the level of openness that the administrator allows and, most of all, how the interaction relates to the learning objectives for the course.

In this chapter, we will review the benefits of structuring a course around collaborative activities such as those found in Forums and in Chat. We will discuss what unique benefits can be found in Chat activities and we will review how to build chat rooms and how to construct productive questions to use in Chat.

Interaction involves collaboration

Some people think of Forums and Chat activities as being interactive but they do not look at the collaborative nature of the activity. In Moodle, the instructor has the opportunity to make all the discussion activities in a place where students can learn to collaborate with each other as they post their papers, read and post in response to their fellow students, and work together in peer reviews of papers and other work.

All interaction in Moodle involves collaboration, at least at a very basic level. So it is, in essence, a focused and purposeful interaction. To be effective, it's important to have an overall goal and measurable outcome for your interaction and/or collaboration. For example, you may say that you'd like to have open office hours in the Chatroom and you can invite students to *drop in* and chat. But what will they do? Why will they do it? Certainly you may be accomplishing the goal of establishing human connections and forging an emotional bond, but that's not really enough.

You need to make a connection to a learning goal. For example, if you put together a synchronous chat room and give it a name, such as Project 1 Topics, you can ask students to drop in and share their topics and their ideas on that topic. They can also share links to resources and also pose questions and insights they might have. Thus, the activity could tie to the outcome of identifying a key topic to study or to a higher-level goal such as creating a collaborative project.

Collaboration and interaction in Moodle can be either synchronous or asynchronous. Asynchronous interaction (discussion boards, forums, wikis) can form the foundation of the course and help develop a viable, thriving learning community. In the previous chapter, we discussed how we can put together a course built around Forums and that the advantages to such arrangements include the ability for students and the instructor to discuss the instructional materials (texts, videos, audio, multimedia presentations, and more) and to share their perceptions and projects. By engaging in a conversation, they develop a sense of community. By sharing work and by examining samples, they learn through emulation and example. There are many effective ways to learn when students interact with each other. In addition, they feel motivated and develop a sense of confidence.

Positive interactions in the forums can motivate students and help them learn from each other. It may take some time obtaining responses to some questions and, in some cases, students may prefer the idea of real-time communication or chat. The advantage of real-time chat is immediacy. You can get immediate answers and you can also share them later by saving a transcript and making it available to team members.

In fact, for students who are used to almost instant communication via text messages or social media such as Google Hangouts or Twitter, the asynchronous communication of a Forum may seem frustratingly slow. They prefer brief, instantaneous communication. So, for students preferring to send and receive quick (and often very brief, if we look at Twitter) text messages, a good solution may be to put together chat solutions. In Moodle, online chat is very easy to implement and it allows students to communicate with each other in real time.

At this point, you may be asking yourself,
Why use Moodle's Chat when we can incorporate Skype, Twitter, BigBlueButton, Google Hangouts, and other well-known third-party synchronous communication solutions? Again, it's a combination of security, control, and convenience. With Moodle 3.0, Chat has more settings and is more flexible and the instructor/administrators have the ability to define groups and to schedule chat times. Above all, it's possible to save the transcripts so that no one misses

anything. Finally, because all the actions take place within the Moodle platform and it does not require access to a cloud-based application, there is a great deal-more security. You do not have to worry about student posts somehow ending up on non-course social media sites.

One caveat to remember with Chats is the fact that students must be scheduled to participate in the chat at the same time. This can cause some issues if your students live in disparate time zones. With careful scheduling, this issue can be overcome.

With text messaging or Chat, students can share ideas and thoughts. They can also send each other files and post presentations, graphics, video, and more. They can react and respond to each other's work and can revise, emend, and expand the work of others. For students used to a web-enhanced world, Chat is ideal.

Uses of Chat

You may wonder why use Moodle's Chat when Skype, MSN Messenger, AOL Instant Messenger, and other large services offer Internet telephony and chat capability, even with video and file transfer abilities.

The answer is simple. By using Moodle's chatroom, you have control of the tools and the transcript and you're able to automatically contact the individuals who are registered in your course. Moodle's chatroom is connected with your courses and so only people who have registered for your course can enter. It is much easier to keep up with assessment and to assign grades for Chat participation with Moodle's convenient integration.

In this chapter, we explore questions such as
What is Chat good for? And How can I achieve success in an online Chat? As Moodle's Chat function is similar to most other chat software, the answers to these questions apply to more than just Moodle.

Test preparation and online study groups

For some students, an online class may seem very isolated. This is especially true for those of us who grew up before the age of online bulletin boards, instant messaging, and short text messages. As midterm and final exam time approaches and the students' stress levels increase, this feeling of isolation can grow. Using chat sessions for review and test preparation can reduce the feeling of isolation and can be an effective teaching method. Also, the chat logs provide a unique learning tool, which you won't get in a face-to-face review session.

Creating study groups

One of the keys to a successful chat session is limiting the number of participants. If you are teaching a large class, consider breaking the class into groups and holding a review session for each group. Moodle enables you to separate any class or specific activity into groups. The members of one group cannot participate in the activities of another group. So, when you separate your class into groups, you've essentially created a separate chat for each group. The groups can be totally separate so that the members of each group cannot see each others' work or even be visible to each other, so that members of one group can see but not participate in the other groups' work. The chat transcripts can be made visible for all students if you'd like. In the case of study groups and other chat topics, be sure to name the chatroom and to tie it to a specific learning objective or course goal.

Groups carried over to other activities

When you create a group in Moodle, it exists at the course level. This means the group can be applied to all activities within the course and not outside.

If you separate the students into groups for a chat and then use those groups in other activities, the students will have the same group in those other activities. Before separating students into groups for a chat, you should consider the effect that the grouping will have on any other activity in the course.

If you want to use different groups for different activities, you will need to either:

- Change the group membership as needed, that is, change the groups as you progress through the course
- Create a second course, enroll your students in the second course, and create alternative groups and activities in that course

Key settings for study groups in Chat

The key settings in the **Editing Chat** window are:

- **Save past sessions**: This determines how long the chat transcript is saved
- **Everyone can view past sessions**: This enables the students to view the transcripts
- **Next chat time**: You may also set the time and dates for chat sessions that repeat themselves.

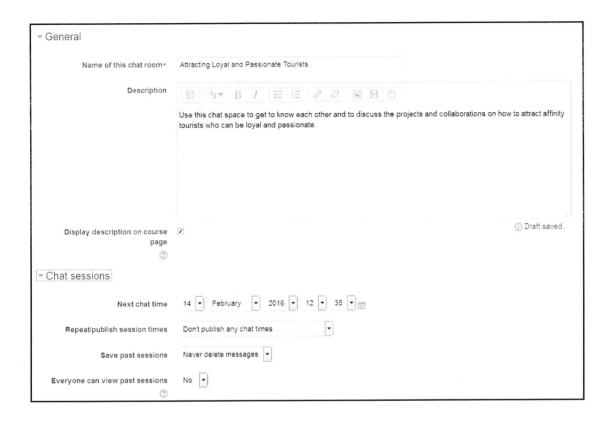

Assigning review topics

If the study group has not worked together before, you might want to jump-start their relationship by assigning each student in the group a different review topic to prepare for the chat. You should also prepare review questions to ask each student during the chat. Remember that, in an online chat, it's very easy for students to *lurk* and watch without participating. You need to be ready to draw them out with questions about the review material that you've assigned.

Kinds of questions

Typing is more difficult than speaking and people naturally take the path of least resistance. Keep your questions open ended and encourage students to elaborate so that they do not give one word answers, which is an easy way out.

In this example on new trends in tourism, students provide their own opinions and suggestions about how to promote a specific beach community.

Notice that the question can be used for students to start sharing ideas that can then be used for collaborating in a project or for posting in a discussion forum. The chat is more informal and, since it's synchronous, it allows for more spontaneity and real-time sharing of ideas.

Reviewing papers and other assignments

Regrettably, the Internet has made plagiarism easier than ever. Moodle can't be used to determine if a paper or passage is plagiarized, but a private chat in Moodle can tell you if a student learned anything from the paper of assignment he/she handed in. The more original a paper, the more the student will remember about it and learn from it. You can schedule a private chat with each student after they've submitted their papers and ask them questions about the subject of their papers.

Keep in mind that chat sessions are not just for sharing verbal content or comments. They are also effective if the instructor incorporates links to resources or if students share links to articles, videos, images, and other pertinent resources.

Creating a one-on-one chat

There are a variety of situations where you might want to chat one-on-one. Reviewing a student's assignment is one of them. Moodle does not offer an obvious way to limit the participants in a chat to just you and one selected student. Just as we used a workaround in Chapter 2, *Instructional Material*, to set up a private forum for one student and the teacher, we need to use a workaround here to set up a private chat. You may set a number of criteria so that the student cannot access the chat until the terms are satisfied.

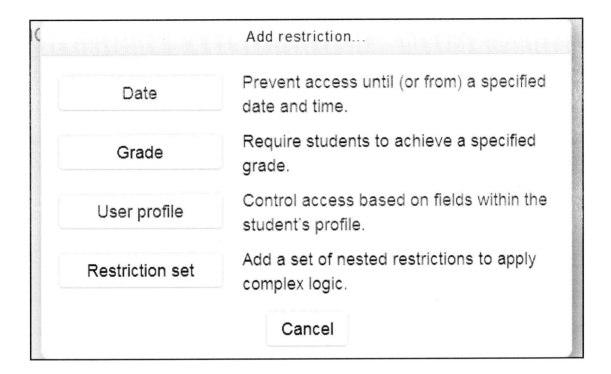

Workaround 1 – Using groups

The workaround for creating a one-on-one forum involves using the Groups feature. Moodle enables you to create a separate chat for each group in a class. We can create a group for every single student in our class and then create a chat with the groups. If we select **Separate groups** for the **Group mode**, we will totally segregate each student into his or her own chat room, where only that student and the teacher can participate and see the transcript. This would be appropriate if students should not see each other's papers. If we select **Visible groups** for the **Group mode**, we will limit the Chatroom to just the student and teacher but other students will be able to see the transcript. This would be appropriate if students are allowed to see other papers.

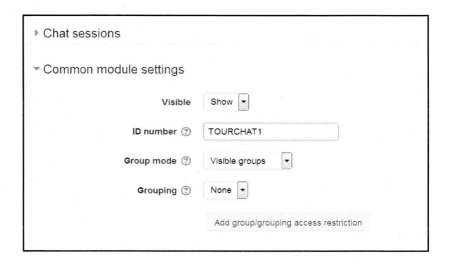

Workaround 2 – Restricting access

Another way to keep a chatroom private is to restrict access by means of groups or user profiles or another set of restrictions that will make sure that only the person you want to chat with will be able to see and/or enter the chat.

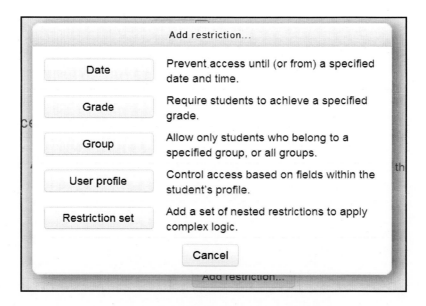

The chat will be hidden from all students who do not fit the criteria.

Guest speakers

Chat gives you a chance to have a guest speaker in your online course. You'll need to create a student-level account for your guest speaker. When you're creating the speaker's account, as a matter of courtesy set the **Email display** setting to **Hide my email address from everyone**, unless your guest speaker explicitly gives permission for students to contact him/her via e-mail.

You will also need the speaker's permission to save the chat session for future viewing. This is to avoid copyright issues. Try to get this in writing from the speaker.

For a good example of a chat transcript featuring a guest speaker, see: `http://nstoneit.com/elearning/wp-content/uploads/2008/06/schoolchat.jpg`.

Including chats from previous classes

The **Save past sessions** setting saves a transcript of each chat session. You can use these transcripts as reference material in your classes. To get the transcript from a past chat into your class, use the **Backup** function to export the chat from the previous class and the **Restore** function to bring it into your current class. You will need admin or manager access to do this since teachers cannot back up or restore user data.

Copying a transcript

The procedure for copying a transcript of a chat is as follows:

1. Enter the past course as a **Teacher** or **Administrator**.
2. From the **Administration** block, select **Chat Administration**.

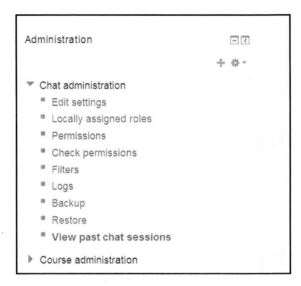

3. On the **Chat Administration** menu, as shown in the next screenshot, select **View past chat sessions**.

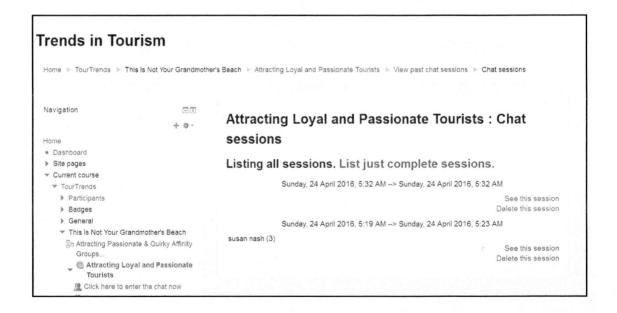

4. Click on the **View past chat sessions** button and then click on **List all sessions**.

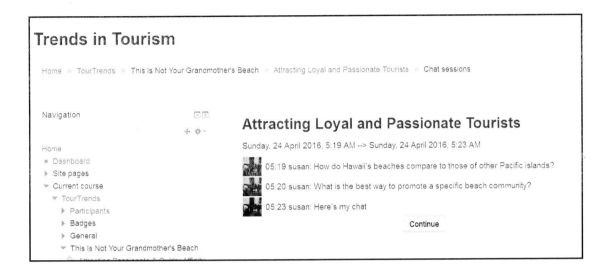

5. Click on **See this session** in the session you are interested in.
6. Copy and paste the session transcript into a Word document.

The **Everyone can view past sessions** setting enables students to view the transcripts of past chats. This means you can save the chat transcripts from previous classes and use them as reference material in the future. However, the very presence of a chat room in your course means that students can enter the chat room at any time and engage in a chat session. How do you include the transcript of a past chat in your course without creating an active chat room? The answer is Moodle's **Override roles** function.

From the **Editing Chat** window, select **Override roles**. By default, the **Talk in a chat** option is checked only for the Student role. Selecting **Prevent** for this capability will disable the student's permission to talk in the chat room, while still allowing them to read chat logs.

Foreign language practice

You can use chatrooms to pair up students with foreign language speakers for language practice. A chat room offers the following advantages for language practice:

- A chat enables students to reach out to another country in ways they might not be able to without the chat.

- A chat's pace is usually faster than most written exercises, yet slower than face-to-face conversation. In a chat, the student has extra, but not too much time, to translate what his/her foreign partner said and to think about what to say next. A chat's pacing makes it a good transition between leisurely-written exercises and fast face-to-face exchanges.
- Chat logs provide material for review and remediation. After the chat, each student can review their own or another student's transcript for grammar, spelling, and vocabulary. For instructions on how to accomplish this, see the *Compiling and reviewing chat transcripts* section later in this chapter.

If you are configuring your chat as a part of a virtual lab or *conversation circle* for a foreign language class, you may wish to also embed apps or include a link to online resources such as dictionaries and translation software. A few include WordReference (`http://www.word reference.com/`) and Google Translate. Google Translate may not be as effective as other programs but it is free.

Preparing for foreign language chat

One of the keys to a successful foreign language chat is preparing the students' vocabulary. Before starting chat, agree upon the topic with your foreign counterpart. Prepare your students by building their vocabulary in that topic. Also, give the students a list of keystrokes for foreign language characters. Feel free to copy the following table for the benefit of your students.

Typing foreign language characters
Hold down the *Alt* key and type the four digits on your keyboard, not the numeric keypad. When you release the *Alt* key, the foreign language character will appear.

Character	Keyboard shortcut
á	*Alt + 0225*
à	*Alt + 0224*
â	*Alt + 0226*
ä	*Alt + 0228*
å	*Alt + 0229*
Á	*Alt + 0193*
Ã	*Alt + 0195*

Ä	*Alt + 0196*
Å	*Alt + 0197*
À	*Alt + 0192*
Â	*Alt + 0194*
æ	*Alt + 0230*
Æ	*Alt + 0198*
ç	*Alt + 0231*
Ç	*Alt + 0199*
ê	*Alt + 0234*
é	*Alt + 0233*
ë	*Alt + 0235*
è	*Alt + 0232*
Ê	*Alt + 0202*
Ë	*Alt + 0203*
É	*Alt + 0201*
È	*Alt + 0200*
ï	*Alt + 0239*
í	*Alt + 0237*
î	*Alt + 0238*
ì	*Alt + 0236*
Í	*Alt + 0205*
Ì	*Alt + 0204*
Î	*Alt + 0206*
Ï	*Alt + 0207*
ñ	*Alt + 0241*
Ñ	*Alt + 0209*
œ	*Alt + 0156*
Œ	*Alt + 0140*

ô	*Alt + 0244*
ö	*Alt + 0246*
ò	*Alt + 0242*
õ	*Alt + 0245*
ó	*Alt + 0243*
ø	*Alt + 0248*
Ó	*Alt + 0211*
Ô	*Alt + 0212*
Õ	*Alt + 0213*
Ø	*Alt + 0216*
Ö	*Alt + 0214*
Ò	*Alt + 0210*
š	*Alt + 0154*
Š	*Alt + 0138*
ú	*Alt + 0250*
ü	*Alt + 0252*
û	*Alt + 0251*
ù	*Alt + 0249*
Ù	*Alt + 0217*
Ú	*Alt + 0218*
Ü	*Alt + 0220*
Û	*Alt + 0219*
ÿ	*Alt + 0255*
Ÿ	*Alt + 0159*
ý	*Alt + 0253*
Ý	*Alt + 0221*
ª	*Alt + 0170*
Þ	*Alt + 0222*

þ	*Alt + 0254*
ƒ	*Alt + 0131*
ß	*Alt + 0223*
µ	*Alt + 0181*
Ð	*Alt + 0208*

Compiling and reviewing chat transcripts

You can take several approaches for reviewing chat logs. One of the easiest approaches is to have students copy a minimum number of lines from their chat logs into an online assignment and edit these in the assignment window. Or you can copy lines from the various chats yourself and compile them into a document that you then ask the students to edit online. This enables you to choose the chat portions that offer the greatest opportunity for learning.

Moodle's `Assignment` module gives you an easy place to present the transcript and instruct the student to edit it.

Copying chat transcripts

In order to copy a chat transcript in Moodle, as you select the text also select the avatars (pictures) of the participants and the time of each post.

You might not want to include the avatars and times in the transcript. To create a copy of the transcript without these, do the following:

Select the part of the chat transcript that you want to copy and follow this procedure:

1. Press *Ctrl + C* or *command + C* to copy.
2. Open a new word processing document. For example, open a new Microsoft Word document.
3. From the **View** menu, select **Normal** (for Word) or **Draft** (for WordPerfect), or **Web Layout** (for OpenOffice). The key is to view the document so that it wraps as few lines as possible. In many word processors, viewing the document in draft mode minimizes the number of lines that are wrapped.
4. From the **Edit** menu, select **Paste special**. At this point, most word processors will give you a dialog box with several choices. Select **Unformatted text**.
5. The chat transcript will be pasted into the word processing document; only the

text is pasted minus the avatars.

6. At this point, if you are in Word, you can use a trick to easily select the times at the beginning of each line. With the *Alt* key held down, draw a rectangle around the characters that you want to select. Your selection can include just the first few words of each line.

7. Delete the selected text. Now you will be left with just the chat participants' names and their dialog.

8. Copy the chat and paste it into the Moodle assignment.

Assigning a chat transcript as an editing exercise

After you have compiled chat transcripts, you can assign students the task of editing them for spelling, grammar, vocabulary, and logic. This is especially useful in a language course after your students have participated in a foreign language chat. You can then compile parts of the chat transcripts into an assignment and have the students find and correct any mistakes that they or their foreign partners made.

Tips for a successful chat

Preparation is the key to a successful chat session. Here are some things that you and your students can do to help make your chats easier and more productive.

Basic chat etiquette

Before the first chat, consider giving your students a short handout with some basic etiquette instructions. You can even include these in the chat announcement. The following are some sample instructions:

1. If you can, wait for the moderator or speaker to ask for your questions.

2. If you want to ask a question and it cannot wait, send a "**?**" and wait for the moderator or speaker to acknowledge you. This is the online equivalent of raising your hand.

3. If you have a comment or observation, send a "**!**" and wait for the moderator or speaker to acknowledge you. When the speaker reaches a good place to pause, he/she will invite you to comment.

4. If you need multiple lines, use "**...**" at the end of a line to indicate there's more to come. Without the "**...**" at the end of a line, other participants assume that you

have finished what you have to say.

5. Just as in an e-mail, uppercase is considered *shouting* and it's more difficult to read than normal mixed case. So avoid it.

6. Give others time to respond to your last message. Sending messages in a rapid sequence, without giving others a chance to respond, can make the chat feel more like an interrogation than a conversation. Also, when you get a response to one of your rapid-fire questions, you might not be able to tell which question the person is responding to.

7. Don't judge the other person on their typing skills. Lots of smart people can't type well. Especially those of us who grew up writing our term papers by hand.

8. Think before hitting *Enter*. The class which you are attending might save the chat transcript for a long time. The person whom you just offended might copy the chat and save it for even longer.

9. Use humor carefully. Without facial expression and tone of voice, humor-especially sarcasm-often translates poorly online. For example, you can say "You gotta be kidding!" in person and make it clear by your tone and expression that you're teasing the other person. Online, it can just as easily be translated as "You're stupid!"

10. If you want to convey an emotion online and you're not confident that your text alone will accurately communicate the mood, consider using *smileys*. These are graphics that you can insert into your text to show the mood of a statement.

11. The table that follows shows you how to type smileys. Note that you type the characters without spaces between them.

Mood	Type this	Mood	Type This
smile	:-)	sad	:-(
big grin	:-D	shy	8-.
wink	;-)	blush	:-I
mixed	:-/	kiss	:-X
thoughtful	V-.	clown	:o)
tongue-out	:-P	black eye	P-I
cool	B-)	angry	8-[
approve	^-)	dead	xx-P
wide eyes	8-)	sleepy	I-.
surprise	8-o	evil	}-]

The codes might be different for different browsers.

12. If you're stepping away from the chat, please send a message to indicate so. Moodle doesn't enable you to set your *status* like many instant message programs, so you need to inform your fellow chatters when you step away and come back to the chat.

Prepare for a definite starting and ending time

"Start and end on time" is a good advice to follow for any class. For an online chat, it is especially important. If a face-to-face class starts late, you can keep the students engaged with conversation until the class starts. Most students will not walk out of the room and, when class does start they will be there ready to participate. If an online chat starts late, you will have no idea if a participant has walked away from his/her computer while waiting for the chat to start and if/when he/she will return. In an online chat, a late starting time can make your students lose interest more easily than in a face-to-face classroom.

Chat is designed to help people engage by being interactive. But if you bore, frustrate, or confuse the students, you could be defeating your learning goals. For that reason, it's a good idea to be sure to select appropriate titles for each chat. In the description, be sure to include a connection to the specific unit, the learning objective, and the outcomes or assessments.

Again, for a synchronous chat, it is possible for it to be ineffective because people are late to the chat or they are quickly bored. You can help prevent this by coming to the chat prepared with some material. This is material which you can use for discussion before the chat begins, but that is not essential for the chat. For example, you might spend a few minutes asking the students about their experience level with online chats or whether their navigation through the course is clear. Or, you may find some interesting or outrageous trivia about the chat subject and quiz the students about it until all the participants have arrived.

Limit the number of participants

Moodle's default Chat module lacks some advanced features that you would use to help manage a large chat. For example, some chat applications enable you to "whisper" to another user, that is, to send them a private message. If a student wants to ask a question to the teacher without interrupting the chat, he/she can whisper that question to the teacher. Some chat applications also have a **Raise your hand** function that enables a student to let the moderator know that he/she wants to speak. And for very large chats, the ability to enable only one person at a time to speak is also very useful. As Moodle's chat module is being developed, these capabilities might be added. But for now, the best way to keep a chat under control is to limit the number of participants.

If you must conduct a chat with a large number of participants, here are a few tips for managing the chat:

- Make the chat window as large as possible so that you can see as much of the chat history and participants as possible.
- The chat should be actively managed by the moderator. The moderator should:
    - Restate the topic at the beginning of the chat.
    - Bring off-topic posts back on topic.
    - Issue a number to each participant and require participants to answer in order, that is, participant number 2 cannot click the **Send** button until participant number 1 has posted a comment and so on.

Prepare a greeting for latecomers

Students might enter the chat at different times. When a student enters a Moodle chat, that person sees only the transcript going forward; the student doesn't see what has already been said in the chat room. If you have a welcome message for students as they enter the chat, you'll need to repeat it each time a student enters the chat. Keep this message in a text file where you can quickly copy and paste it into your chat window.

If your greeting is several paragraphs long, you should be aware that Moodle's chat window does not recognize the *Enter* character. Therefore if you paste two or more paragraphs into the chat window, they will be recognized as one long paragraph. Instead, use *Shift + Enter* to create hard-line breaks between the paragraphs.

Focus

Chatting online requires more effort than talking. Limit the chat session to one specific topic or activity and stick to it. Students should come prepared to discuss one topic or complete one task only. As the moderator, you should be prepared to keep the chat on topic. Unless brainstorming and expanding, the topic is part of the chat's goals and you should respond to off-topic postings by bringing them back on topic. This lends structure to the chat session and helps students stay focused.

Insert HTML

You can insert HTML code into your chat. This is useful for sharing links, embedding graphics, and formatting text in your chat. To insert a link, just type the web address. In a chat, links that you type become automatically clickable.

You can insert images by placing them into the standard HTML image tag. If the image is on the Web, include the full link to the image.

Summary

In this chapter, we discussed the fact that Moodle enables students to learn from each other through interaction and collaboration. We also looked at the advantages of chat over asynchronous forums and reviewed the fact that the chat allows students to have quick feedback and to feel they are a part of a learning community as they share their perspectives, respond to questions, engage in peer review, and share text, graphics, and media files in order to develop collaborative projects. In addition, they can feel they are gathering information for projects or assessments and thus the chat can help them obtain information, as well as to organize it so that it ties to the learning objectives. After the chat session has concluded, transcripts can be edited and used as course material and conversation can proceed at a leisurely pace. This gives participants time to think.

Moodle 3.0 offers much flexibility with respect to chat because it allows you to incorporate access to applications that students already know and use and which have a great deal of functionality. However, the advantage of using Moodle's built-in chat is enhanced security, as well as the ability to easily save and share transcripts. Also, the Moodle mobile app supports the chat feature, which makes it easy to accommodate students who like to use their smartphones and tablets for working on their courses.

The key to using these advantages is preparation. Prepare your students by ensuring that they know Chatroom etiquette and how to use the software. Prepare yourself by having material ready to copy and paste into the chat. Also, everyone should be prepared to focus on the goals and subject of the chat. More than any other online activity, chat requires that the teacher take on a leader's role and guide the students to a successful learning experience.

Assessment

Assessment means different things to different people. Some think of it as a series of quizzes and tests. Others tend to think of it as essays and projects. Others even think of a portfolio that reflects all the work that a student has done in a course. What do all these ideas have in common? All require the student to perform in some way that reflects the course goals and objectives. Finally, assessments are ways to determine whether the course outcomes have been met. While many people tend to look at assessment with a certain level of trepidation, negative emotions are not necessary; in fact, they are counterproductive. In this chapter, we discuss how to create assessments in Moodle and cover the ways to make assessment a positive cornerstone in the overall learning experience.

The purpose of assessment

The main purpose of assessment is to determine if the course goals and learning objectives are being met. For that reason, assessment is extremely important because it helps you determine how effective your learning strategy, course design, and course materials are. While it's fairly easy to say that assessment is just about testing knowledge, the process is much more complicated than that. It is very important to tie the learning objectives to the assessments so that you know that what you are assessing really does demonstrate learning.

In addition to making sure that your students are achieving the course goals and learning objectives, assessment can also be very motivating. It's often encouraging for students to see that they are making progress and also to receive recognition for their achievements.

Assessment can also be effective for encouraging teams and individuals who are collaborating on a project. If they see that their team members are completing their training and succeeding, they are often encouraged to participate as well. Competition can often be a very good thing.

Assessment and your learning objectives

As you select your assessments, make sure that you cover all your learning objectives. It is often very helpful to map your assessments to your learning objectives. The sequence is often very important as well. Start with the first learning objective that you have listed and then map it to an assessment. Move down the list through all your learning objectives and make sure that you have an assessment that corresponds to each one. As you are mapping the assessments, also be sure that the difficulty level is appropriate. For example, if you require students to identify key terms, a multiple choice quiz could be appropriate. If you are asking them to create a plan, an essay or a collaborative activity such as a group project done in **Workshop** could work.

Types of assessments

Matching the learning objective with the appropriate assessment can help you make sure that your students are able to demonstrate that they've achieved mastery of the concepts or skills required.

For lower-level knowledge such as definitions and identification of items, it is often good to use quizzes. For higher-level cognitive levels (which correspond to higher levels on Bloom's taxonomy), you may ask your students to write essays, complete short-answer questions, and even to participate in a workshop in order to complete a collaborative activity.

Keys to successful assessment

The following questions have to be asked in order to determine the key to a successful assessment: How can you determine how and where students are learning? What are the best measures and how can you use them?

In an online course, you have many opportunities to create assessments and mini-assessments that can help students develop a sense of confidence. They will also become more aware of what they are learning and how their knowledge is growing over time.

Here are a few guidelines for creating effective assessments and for deciding how and where to offer them within Moodle:

- Assessments must be connected in an integral way with the course goals and standards.
- Assessments must be aligned with all the instructional content and activities so

that the information provided directly relates to the desired learning outcomes.

- Assessments must ask students to perform tasks that are on the same level as the learning objectives. For example, if a learning objective involves identification or definition, then the assessment should correspond on the same level. This is an aspect of assessment that is often overlooked by course designers, but thankfully, with forethought and consideration, it is fairly easy to accommodate.

- Assessments should ask students to perform in a manner appropriate to the course outcomes. This point reinforces what was mentioned earlier. For example, if the outcome states that, at the end of a course, the student should be able to write a persuasive essay that supports its primary thesis with evidence, then the assessment should involve writing. In this case, a multiple choice test or quiz would not be the ideal approach to assessment because it would be testing something besides one's ability to formulate, defend, and argue.

- Information upon which assessments are based must be available in a timely and transparent fashion so that students can study and practice.

- Practice tests, quizzes, and other assessments should mirror the actual assessment that they will be asked to perform.

- Practice assessments should have a companion discussion forum in order to enable students to share strategies for studying effectively, solving problems, and time management.

- Practice assessments allow students to replicate the conditions under which they will be taking an exam. For example, if the quiz is timed, then the practice quiz should have time constraints as well.

- Assessments should be designed to give students a chance to build self-efficacy, which relates to a positive self-concept and a belief in one's ability to perform successfully.

Taking the fear out of assessment

If you ask students what they dread most in an online course, the answer almost invariably has to do with quizzes, tests, and other assessments. After they express their test anxiety, students usually add that they fear the unknown and dread the idea that they might be all alone in a course with no one to ask for help.

If you use Moodle to design your course, you'll find that you can help allay student fears about assessment. They will have clear, predictable assessments, with many chances to practice so they do not have to fear the unknown. With discussion forums, Moodle gives you the chance to create a place where students can support each other and create "study buddies."

Moodle is ideal for creating assessments that build confidence and help measure whether course outcome objectives are being met. Moodle is ideal because its forum-based structure allows students to take practice assessments, share their experiences, and learn from each other. For example, it is possible to post a practice quiz and then to let students post their thoughts about the best way to approach the questions.

If the assessment involves writing an assignment such as an essay, you can open a forum in which you ask your students to post drafts of an essay and then to respond to each other's drafts with constructive comments. If you are asking your students to turn in a portfolio, the work they have done for the course, then you can set up a forum in which each student creates a portfolio and then goes through and evaluates a fellow student's work.

By using the forum space as a place to let students post work, discuss it, and to practice any quizzes or tests they'll have to do later, you're creating a friendly, supportive environment, and you're helping your students feel confident in their ability to perform. Further, you're giving them a chance to practice and to feel connected to other people in the course. This will help them develop positive belief in themselves and they will have a higher likelihood of success.

Performance anxiety often has to do with the fear of the unknown or, worse, the fear of public humiliation and shame. Performance anxiety can be exacerbated by the fear of the unknown. One good way to counter performance anxiety is to remove the unknown, that is, spelling out what the students are going to encounter, and giving many examples as well as opportunities to practice.

Successful performance in assessment often has to do with what psychologist

Mihaly Csikszentmihalyi has referred to as "flow." *Flow* is a highly pleasurable state of mind that occurs when you are so absorbed in your activity that you lose all sense of time and space. Think of playing tennis. There are clearly defined rules of the game and your goals are clear. As you focus on producing perfect strokes, connecting with the ball, and directing it to precisely the place you'd like it to go, your levels of concentration and absorption in the process are so heightened that you've merged action and awareness. The cognitive and the physical come together and you're feeling a sense of joy, connection, and above all a profound sense of satisfaction.

One of the keys to achieving flow is to understand what is expected from you. In tennis, knowing what to do occurs through practice. In an online course, for the issue of assessment, the same concepts apply. The key is to provide many opportunities for practice.

Assessment with quizzes and distributed practice

Once you have determined the ideal instructional strategy for your course that will involve a certain number of assessments, you can start the process of building them in Moodle. For learning outcomes that involve identification, definition, and explanation of concepts and key terms, a quiz is often a very effective assessment tool. Fortunately, Moodle makes it convenient to create a quiz that ties directly to the **Gradebook**. It also allows you to put in time constraints and to allow students to retake and repeat the quiz for practice and encourage proficiency. One useful technique for students in the online environment is the concept of distributed practice.

Distributed practice is when a student practices a skill or knowledge during many sessions that are short in length and distributed over time. For example, if you're teaching a language course, you might practice every day for one week on a list of vocabulary words. That would be distributed practice. But even more effective than that would be repeating that practice once a week for the next few weeks.

Advantages and limitations of distributed practice

Students who use distributed practice learn more material and remember the material longer as compared to students who cram. This is due to the following reasons:

- It's easier for students to maintain motivation and focus for short spans of time rather than for an all-night study session.
- Short practice sessions prevent mental and physical tiredness. Fatigue interferes with memory and reasoning and reduces the ability to focus.

Research indicates that we continue to learn and process information that we study even after the study period has ended. If our brains were ovens, you could say we continue to *bake* the knowledge for a while even after the heat has been shut off. The more practice sessions we engage in, the more we experience this effect

We may not be totally aware of the cognitive processes at work, but they are occurring nonetheless. For example, your mind is creating categories, or schemata, in order to organize the new knowledge. You are practicing retrieving information in your long-term memory by creating pathways in your working memory. Finally, you are making connections to your prior knowledge or past experience that will help you make sense of the knowledge and relate it to the world.

Several factors affect how efficiently distributed practice works:

Factor	Effect on distributed practice
Length of the practice session	The shorter the better. It should be just long enough to cover the material but not too long that it fatigues the student.
Time between practice sessions	Research shows that, at first, the time between sessions should be short enough so that students don't forget the material between practice sessions. As the students gain proficiency and confidence with the material, the time between sessions can be increased. There are no hard-and-fast rules. As a teacher, you must use your judgment and monitor the students' performance, adjusting the time between sessions as needed.
Time period over which practice sessions are distributed	The longer the better. Keep returning to the material until the students master it. Students might demonstrate mastery by performing well on the quizzes you give them or by using the material in an activity such as writing a paper or participating in a forum.

With all this talk of the advantages of distributed practice, there are some situations where massed practice (a long study or work session) is better. For example, when you're writing a paper, you often reach a point where you are accomplishing several things at once. You are writing a section now, you have your next few points in mind, you have recalled the next few pieces of information that you need to use, and you know where the piece that you are working on fits into the overall organization of the paper. At that point, you do not want to be interrupted. But if you are interrupted, if you are using a building block approach, it's often very effective.

You have achieved the sense of *flow* that we mentioned earlier in this chapter. Writers, programmers, artists, and people who do creative work know that, sometimes, the best way to be productive is to exert a sustained and uninterrupted effort. For each learning situation, you must consider which would give better results: distributed practice or sustained effort.

Opening and closing quizzes at predetermined times

The **Editing Quiz** window contains settings that enable you to determine when a quiz becomes available and unavailable to students:

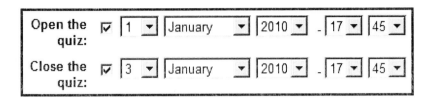

Remember that the show/hide setting determines whether a student can see an item in the course. So, even when a quiz is closed, students can see it listed in the course. The setting can be used in the following ways:

- When the quiz is open or closed, or if the course developer has set it to **Show**. The student will see the quiz listed on the course's home page.
- When the quiz is open or closed, or if the course developer has set it to **Hidden.** The student will not see the quiz listed on the course's home page.

If a student selects a closed quiz, he/she sees the quiz's description and a message stating when the quiz will open (or when it's closed).

Indicating that a quiz is closed

If you're going to close a quiz until a given date, will you allow the student to stumble into the quiz and discover that it is closed until a given date? Or will you indicate to the student that the quiz is closed? You have several options.

In the following screenshot, you can see that Moodle tells the student: **The quiz will not be available until: Friday, 1 January, 2010, 5:45 PM**. However, that information is not very prominent. Consider using the first line of the quiz's description to explain that the quiz is closed until the open date, so it's the first thing the student reads after selecting the quiz:

```
Moodle Solutions ▶ QuizSolutions ▶ Quizzes ▶ Closed Quiz

  Closed Quiz

  This quiz exists only to show what a closed quiz appears like to the student. Check
  back in 2010 if you'd like to take the quiz!


              Grading method: Highest grade

    The quiz will not be available until: Friday, 1 January 2010, 05:45 PM
```

You can use a label on the course's homepage to indicate that the quiz is closed, like this:

```
The quiz below will open when we finish this topic, on January 1, 2010.
☑ End-of-unit Quiz
```

You can also hide the quiz until it's time for the student to take it.

Using quizzes for frequent self-assessment

Self-assessment is the ability of a student to observe, analyze, and judge his/her performance based on criteria that you supply. At its best, self-assessment also means that the student can determine how to improve his/her performance. Supplying the students with quizzes that they can take themselves fulfills the first part of that goal. Using feedback during the quizzes helps fulfill the second.

Self-assessments are typically not graded. The goal of a self-assessment is usually not to achieve a grade but to practice for a graded activity.

Adding self-assessment to your course has several advantages for you and the students:

- First, self-assessments are a chance for students to become more actively involved in their learning.

- Second, students learn to identify their errors as they make them, assuming the self-assessment quiz provides immediate feedback. This feedback during self-assessment reduces the errors students make *when it counts*, that is, when they are being graded.
- Third, self-assessments build students' confidence and make them more independent learners and, as a teacher, your workload is reduced by self-assessment quizzes that provide feedback because they reduce the need for you to provide feedback yourself.

Further, with a self-assessment element, you are able to build the students self-efficacy and "I can do it" sense of confidence.

1. Follow these steps. First, click on **Grade Exceptions** so that your students' self-assessment does not affect their official grade.

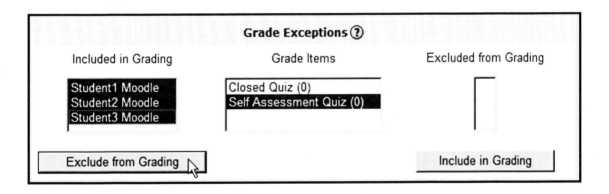

2. And then, select **Exclude from Grading**. This excludes that activity from the selected students' overall grade.

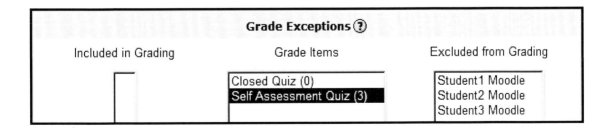

3. However, note that for the other activity in this course, the **Closed Quiz**, all of the students' grades will still be included in the **Gradebook**.

Grade Exceptions ⑦		
Included in Grading	Grade Items	Excluded from Grading
Student1 Moodle Student2 Moodle Student3 Moodle	Closed Quiz (0) Self Assessment Quiz (3)	

When using this method to exclude self-assessment quizzes from the **Gradebook**, remember that, if a student joins your course late, you'll need to return to the **Grade Exceptions** page and exclude that student's self-assessment quiz grades from the **Gradebook**.

Making a quiz – a learning tool

In an online environment, immediate error correction almost always takes the form of feedback provided by the learning system. The feedback is a response to a student's answer to a quiz question. It often refers back to the correct response and also provides a connection to the course content.

Questions must be specific

Immediate feedback is one of the strengths of an e-learning system. One of the weaknesses of an online environment is that the teacher can't ask why the student picked an incorrect answer. The teacher cannot immediately ask the student to discover exactly what information he/she is missing. For example, this quiz question asks questions about two items; in what order should you add the chemicals, and when should they be heated? Break this question into two more specific questions and then you can design appropriate error corrections for each question:

1. In what order should you add the chemicals?
2. After the addition of which chemical should the mixture be heated?

Online quiz questions must be very specific for immediate error correction to work online. There must be no doubt what item of knowledge is being measured. As feedback is a response to a quiz question, the questions and remedial information must be carefully matched. The quiz question must be specific enough to measure with certainty what piece of information the student is missing.

Adding feedback to quiz questions

Moodle enables you to create several different kinds of feedback for a quiz. There are two kinds of feedback:

- You can create feedback for the entire quiz that changes with the student's score. This is called **Overall feedback** and uses a feature called **Grade boundary**.
- You can create feedback for a question no matter what the student's score on that question is. All students receive the same feedback. This is called **General feedback** that every question can have.

In order to see how the screen looks for feedback, refer to the second screenshot in the next section. The type of feedback that you can create for a question varies with the type of question.

Feedback for a multiple choice question

In a multiple choice question, you can create feedback for correct, partially correct, or incorrect responses. If a response has a value of 100%, it is considered completely correct and the student receives all of the points for that question. However, a response can have a value of less than 100%. For example, if a question has two correct responses, you could give each response a value of 50%. In this case, each response is partially correct. The student needs to choose both responses to receive the full point value for the question. Any question with a percentage value between 0 and 100 is considered partially correct.

A response can also have a negative percentage value. Any response with a percentage value of less than zero is considered an incorrect response.

Choosing a response with a value of 100% will display the feedback under **Feedback for any correct answer**. Choosing any response with a point value between 0 and 100% displays the feedback under **Feedback for any partially correct answer**. Choosing any response with a zero or negative percentage displays the feedback under **Feedback for any incorrect answer**. Each response can display its own feedback. This type of feedback is called **Response Feedback** or just **Feedback**.

The following screenshot shows **Overall feedback** with grade boundaries. Students who score 90-100% on the quiz receive the first feedback: **You're a geography wizard!** Students who score 80-89.99% receive the second feedback: **Very good!**:

```
Overall feedback ②

Grade boundary:  100%
      Feedback:  [You're a geography wizard! Try the Advanced Geography Trivia quiz.]
Grade boundary:  [90]
      Feedback:  [Very good! Try the Intermediate Geography Trivia quiz.]
Grade boundary:  [80]
      Feedback:  [Not bad. Try another Geography Trivia quiz and see how you do.]
Grade boundary:  [70]
      Feedback:  [You're not ready to move up to the next level. Keep trying!]
Grade boundary:  [          ]
      Feedback:  [          ]
Grade boundary:  0%

            [ Save changes ]   [ Cancel ]
```

The following screenshot shows the screen for multiple-choice questions that use several kinds of feedback. You're seeing this question from the course creator's point of view, not the student's. You can see the following text under **General Feedback: The truth is, most New Yorkers have never even thought about the "missing Fourth Avenue" issue**. After the question is scored, every student sees this feedback, no matter their score.

Below that, you can see **Choice 1** through **Choice 4** containing feedback for each response. This feedback is customized to the response. For example, if a student selects **Sixth Avenue**, the feedback is **Nope, that name is taken. Sixth is also known as the "Avenue of the Americas."**

Near the bottom of the page, under **Feedback for any incorrect answer**, you can see the feedback the system gives if the student selects one of the incorrect responses. In this case, we use the feedback to tell the student what the correct response is.

There is no feedback under **Feedback for any correct answer** or **Feedback for any partially correct answer**. Those options are useful when you have multiple responses that are correct or responses that are partially correct. In this case, only one response is correct and all other responses are incorrect:

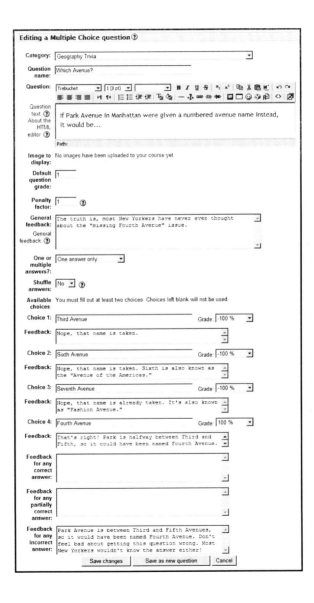

Feedback for a numeric question

The next screenshot shows feedback for a question with a numeric answer. Note that **General Feedback** explains how the question is solved. This feedback is displayed to everyone after answering the question, even those who answered correctly. You might think that, if the student answered correctly, he/she doesn't need this explanation. However, if the student guessed, or used a different method from that given in **General feedback**, explaining the solution can help the student to learn from the question.

For a question that requires a numeric answer, the student types in a number for the answer. This means the student could enter literally any number. It would be impossible to create customized feedback for every possible answer because the possibilities are infinite. However, you can create customized feedback for a reasonable number of answers. In this question, I've created responses for the most likely incorrect answers. After I've given this test to the first group of students, I'll need to review their responses for the most frequent incorrect answers. If there are any that I haven't covered, I'll need to add them to the feedback for this question.

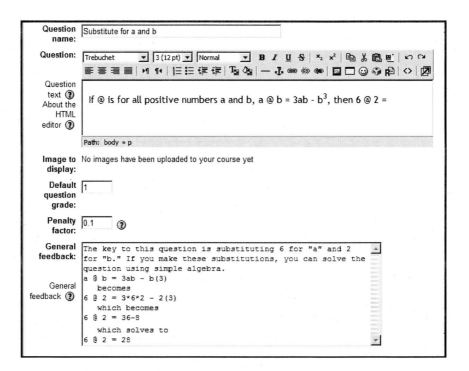

In the following screenshot, note that each response has customized feedback. **Answer 1** is correct. **Answer 2** would be the result of switching the two numbers while trying to solve the problem. As this is a likely error, I've included feedback just for that answer, explaining the error the student made. **Answer 3** is the result of interpreting b^3 as b *times* 3 instead of b *cubed*. This is also a likely error, so I've included feedback for that answer. **Answer 4** is a wildcard and applies if the student submitted any answer other than the three above.

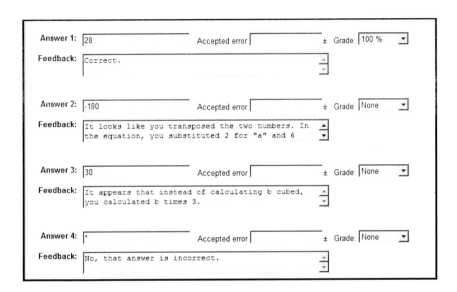

Reinforcing expertise with timed quizzes

Timed quizzes are an example of teaching using a strategy called **time trials**. Time trials can be used to:

- **Measure** a student's competence at the beginning of a learning unit
- **Build** a student's confidence with the knowledge or skill
- **Test** a student's mastery at the end of a learning unit

Chapter 1, *Developing an Effective Online Course*, has a section that explains the theory behind time trials in more detail. In general, you should use time trials to build mastery of existing skills and knowledge, and not to build new knowledge. Time trials are a confidence-building technique.

When a student selects a timed quiz, the system displays the time limit for the quiz. You might also want to state the time limit in the quiz's description, as shown in the following screenshot:

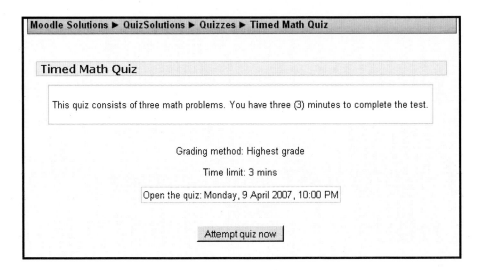

When the student selects **Attempt quiz now**, the student is reminded that the quiz has a time limit:

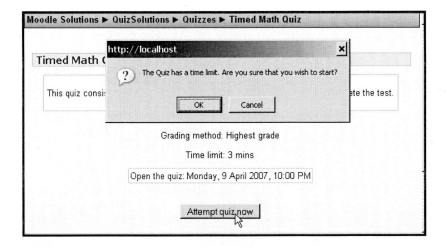

After the student selects **OK**, the quiz displays a timer that appears in a separate floating window, as shown in the following screenshot:

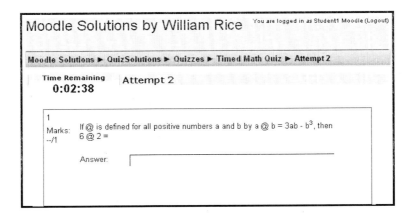

Adding a **Time Limit** to a quiz is a matter of changing one setting on the **Editing Quiz** page, as highlighted in the following screenshot:

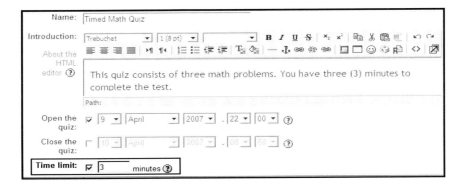

Assessment and motivation

You might not think that knowing that you're going to have to take a test or a quiz would be motivating but let's think about it. Knowing that you'll have to perform can be a great motivator for completing tasks, and also for maintaining focus and concentration.

Also, successfully completing an assessment can help build a sense of mastery, and thus build confidence. In that way, assessment can help motivate learners.

According to psychologists Edwin Locke and Gary Latham, appropriate goal-setting can be very motivating as well, especially if the goals are designed well. They found that goals are motivating as long as there is sufficient clarity, commitment, feedback, challenge, and task complexity. As you design your course, you can incorporate Locke and Latham's findings in setting goals that involve assessment that fit the criteria described.

You can also use quizzes to engage students and keep their interest high. In addition to *Did You Know* choice activities, you can create *Check Your Knowledge* quizzes that engage students.

As you create knowledge-check self-assessments, be sure to use multiple choice and, in the response, provide a link to the location of the answer and a brief explanation of the correct response.

Frequent self-assessment

For assessment to be effective, it should be consistent and also frequent enough for individuals to continue to see how they are achieving the learning objectives or where they may need to study more.

Self-assessment is most effective when there is appropriate automated feedback and also enough flexibility to be able to return to areas where there are gaps in skills or knowledge. The assessment does not necessarily have to be adaptive per se, but with frequent self-assessment one can diagnose potential problems early on in the learning process and can avoid painful and demotivating failures later.

Self-generating certificates upon successful completion of assessment activities

The Certificate plugin is a very useful program that you can configure so that it issues a PDF certificate when the learner completes with a passing score (which you select) for the activities that you've selected.

This plugin allows you to customize the PDF to a certain degree and to select from four pre-designed options. You may include the name of the course, the date, and also the name of the organization awarding the certificate.

You can download the plugin from this site: `https://moodle.org/plugins/mod_certi ficate`.

If you are using Moodle 3.0 or higher, you can use this link: `https://moodle.org/plugins/download.php/9988/mod_certificate_moodle30_2015111601.zip`.

Setting up the Gradebook

To get started with setting up your **Gradebook**, go to the course **Administration** navigation menu. Click on **Grade administration**.

Then, click **Gradebook setup**. This is under **User report** and then under **Setup**. You'll see the different assignments and assessment items that you have included in the course. In this case, you'll see the activity that you put in your **Workshop**. It falls under **Essays**.

If you want to add categories for your assessments and also additional grade items, you can do so here.

You can also customize the grade settings. It is useful to customize grade settings so that they correspond to the grading scale for the course. You can also use the categories to tie them to learning objectives and desired course outcomes.

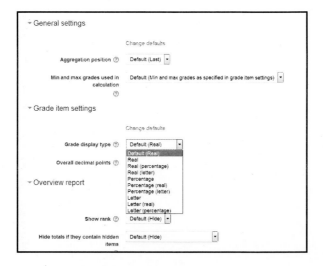

Finally, Moodle 3.0 allows you to create an **Overview report** that gives you a view of all the assessments and student performance. It is a useful *one-stop-shop* approach that allows you to see at a glance whether your students are achieving the learning objectives for the course:

Badges

Badges are digital images that are small, compact, and can be displayed on the Moodle site and also in social media sites, such as Facebook, LinkedIn, or their blogs. They are a great way to demonstrate a skill set or competency, and they can motivate students to complete the course or a program in order to obtain the badge.

The Mozilla Open Badges program (at `http://openbadges.org/`) has a free **Open Badges Backpack** (at `https://backpack.openbadges.org/backpack/login`), which allows individuals to store and display their badges.

To work with the badges, the administrator should go to **Administration | Site administration | Badges | Badges settings**.

To create a new badge, simply click the link and then in the screen complete the details. Note that you can add a photograph to customize the appearance of your badge.

After you click **Create badge**, you'll see the screen that allows you to further customize the badge. Notice that the graphic that you uploaded appears in the **Badge details** section. You may wish to have a badge image that represents the topic or one that contains text and an icon that includes the name and logo of the institution. Both are very effective, depending on your purposes.

Alternatively, you can go to **Default badge issuer** and set the name and email address of the issuer, which should be the name of the organization. If you want to connect to external backpacks such as the Mozilla Open Badges backpack, you should choose **Enable connection to external backpacks**.

If you would like the instructors to be able to manage badges, please enable **Enable course badges.**

The administrator can grant permissions so that managers, course creators, teachers, and non-editing teachers can award and customize the badges for the student.

Summary

In this chapter, we have seen how to use Moodle's Quiz module to create self-assessment and learning experiences. Some of the features we explored are:

- Opening and closing quizzes at predetermined times
- Setting up the **Gradebook**
- Feedback for quizzes, questions, and individual responses to questions
- Timed quizzes
- Using assessment for motivation and engagement
- Setting up **Badges** that are issued upon successful completion of the assessment

There are several other features that you can use to make quizzes a good learning experience. For example, you can use the settings for **Attempts allowed** and **Each attempt builds on the last** to enable students to try a quiz several times. After each attempt, the student can retain the correct answers and work at the wrong answers. You can use **Adaptive mode** to create questions that allow multiple attempts immediately after the student has entered an answer and change their feedback according to the student's answer. I encourage you to explore these, and other, features. With the right approach, perhaps we can change things enough so that the words "test" and "quiz" no longer intimidate students but are, instead, something that they look forward to.

5
Lesson Solutions

One of the most challenging aspects of course development often involves simply determining how to select and organize your material. It is very important to be strategic about the type of material you select. Needless to say, every item used in your course should tie directly to course outcomes, and you should make sure that all your items are used in some way. Beyond that, putting the material in your course can feel fairly confusing. Fortunately, Moodle makes it easy to select, incorporate, and organize your content. Moodle also helps you lead students through the material in a way that will maximize the chances of them finishing your course and successfully achieving learning outcomes. This is possible because, in Moodle 3.0 and beyond, adaptive learning has been incorporated and the student can progress to different parts of the course. Depending on their performance in assessment.

In this chapter, we will discuss the best way to organize your course content into Lessons, along with how to build Lessons using Moodle's unique capacity to let you use and reuse your materials and to arrange and rearrange them. So, with that in mind, prepare to develop a strategy for creating Lessons that can consist of many different elements, which could include readings, practice quizzes, questions for reflection, media, and peer interactions (discussions and student reviews).

You'll learn how to select content so that it contains the appropriate depth, breadth, and level for your students. You'll also learn the best way to organize the material so that the sequence keeps the students on track and allows them to develop successful learning strategies so that they perform well in their outcome assessments. Finally, this chapter will show you how Moodle's object-oriented philosophy of design allows you to go back and update, refine, revise, and retool your course.

Moodle's Lesson activity simplifies your life as an instructional designer, instructor, or Moodle administrator. The Lesson activity gives you a chance to create a place where you can guide the students through the content and the learning assessments. In Moodle 3.0, the focus is on adaptive learning and, with Lesson's two main page types (question pages and content pages), you can direct the student to the content they need, based on their performance in the question pages.

Before we go any further, it is worthwhile to take a moment to clarify Lessons in Moodle. The principal differentiator between a Lesson and another activity module in Moodle is the fact that it is adaptive. The teacher can manually direct students to different parts of the Lesson depending on the responses. Basically, the teacher sends the student to an appropriate page. This process can be automated as well by referring students to different pages based on their performance in a question page.

Selecting and sequencing content for Lessons

In this section, we'll discuss the best way to select content for your Lessons and how to arrange it so that the students naturally progress towards the kinds of competence they need to demonstrate when they get ready for their final assessments.

Create conditions for learning

Everyone has experienced the pain of a bad lecture when there is just absolutely nothing that reaches out and captures your imagination. You squirm, you daydream, and then, when it's over, you can't recall a single thing that was said. In that situation, you can safely say that not much learning took place, not just because the delivery might have been ineffectual, but even more compellingly because the speaker failed to connect with their audience.

Educational psychologist Robert Gagne studied the problem of developing ideal learning conditions and, after years of research, published his findings in a book titled *Conditions of Learning* released in 1965. Basically, he discovered that to create ideal learning conditions, there are nine instructional events that must take place. The first event, which he describes as *gaining attention*, is critical. If you intellectually stimulate the learners, you're activating receptors in their brain and they are more likely to pay attention.

Once you've gained their attention, you should develop activities that will do the following:

- Inform learners of objectives and create levels of expectation
- Stimulate recall of prior learning that relates to your course objectives
- Present instructional content
- Guide your students by creating categories and sequences
- Encourage performance and practice
- Provide feedback (either automatically or personally)
- Assess performance
- Apply knowledge to a job or other activity

Gagne's *instructional events* are not set in stone, but they are very useful as you put your course together. Notice that they are heavily weighted towards performance, which is not too surprising as Gagne was a resolute behaviorist. Other theorists such as Vygotsky might lean more heavily toward social learning and put more emphasis on discussion forums. Moodle's Lesson activity is in many ways the embodiment of "instructional events" and can be very effective as well as engaging and fun to develop.

Employ scaffolding

Lessons employ a building block approach, which means that the student applies the knowledge obtained in one unit to learn the concept or skill in the next. This is, in essence, what we often refer to as scaffolding. Scaffolding is a concept that was developed by Bruner (1975), who used Vygotsky's notions of social and imitative learning in order to explain how people learn from each other in groups and classrooms. Vygotsky held the belief that children learn as they observe teachers and others and, as they adopt practices, they are coached by others to modify their behaviors until they conform to the norm.

Bruner took the idea further and proposed that a good way to help students learn is to have a model (a teacher) perform the activity and then assist the student until they are able to perform independently and freely. Bruner thought of the support that is gradually taken away as *scaffolding*. If you learned to ride a bicycle as a child, you probably used training wheels, so it might be more comfortable to think of this as a *training wheel* approach.

At any rate, wherever and whenever you can, let your students see partially worked problems and work on the problems with them. Peers can also be training wheels or scaffolding for each other as well, as they provide partial solutions, model essays, and partially solved problems in anticipation of being able to do things independently.

Use chunking to help build concepts

Have you ever felt utterly lost in a maze of too much information? Have you heard anyone remarking that they couldn't see the forest for the trees? In each case, the problem was that of too many small bits of information and not enough large organizing sets or categories.

To address that problem, educational psychologists have developed a concept they call *chunking*, which is basically grouping small items into sets. Essentially, you are mentally recoding low-information content and grouping it together. Ideally, the total number of units will decrease and what you'll be left with is a small number of high-information "chunks". Chunks are easier to work with than thousands of individual pieces, just as it's easier to pick up a necklace than a thousand individual beads.

The Lesson activity has, at its core, the concept of chunking. It allows you to put materials together that relate to each other and then, once the knowledge or skill has been demonstrated, it directs you to a different level. In the assessments, students use the information they've acquired and which they have available in their working memory to connect to prior knowledge and experiences, which they apply to new content.

As you develop your content, think of ways to organize, classify, and categorize to help students access and retrieve information using their working memory. Keep in mind that these are good activities to employ early in the Lesson as you seek to help students master the lower-level and foundational cognitive tasks such as identify, define, and describe.

Get students involved early

Learning requires risk-taking. When you ask students to be self-guided and to work through a Lesson, they are engaging in an emotional and psychological risk. But why make students take these risks? Why make them introduce themselves, respond to questions, and interact?

While it's true that some students will feel a certain amount of discomfort as they make themselves vulnerable, the rewards for intellectual and emotional risk-taking are very high. They will feel a sense of affiliation and the essentially dehumanizing e-learning space will become more human and more socially relevant to their lives.

Another key consideration is that students are able to practice higher-level cognitive tasks in the discussion board area. They can evaluate, analyze, and synthesize topics on a deeper level through intellectual interaction with peers. With Moodle 3.0's social media-friendly approach, students can easily incorporate their content from the cloud, which can include photos, blog posts, videos, and audio.

Keep it lively

Gaining attention is something that you'll need to do throughout the class. Students will constantly need to be stimulated, refreshed, and refocused. Not only will you stimulate the receptors in their brains, you'll also help them formulate their own conversation with the content. As for questions in their minds, be sure to relate the content to something practical and relevant-in the world, in their lives, in their prior knowledge-and then encourage them to discuss and debate.

There are many strategies for keeping it lively. One is to include interesting content in the discussion area. Another is to include instructional material that is both thought provoking and that connects to the learners' own experience and, in doing so, incorporates prior knowledge. And finally, it is always a good idea to find a way to make the learner really care. Engage the learners' emotions and, when doing so, be sure to do so in a positive and supportive way.

Keeping it lively not only keeps their attention, it also motivates students to return to the course and will help them maintain a high level of enthusiasm.

Keep focused

There are a number of ways to keep students focused on what you want them to learn. The key is to mix it up and not repeat the same attention-getting tactics or you'll risk having students totally tune out. Try many different strategies-add points, add a video snippet, interject a question, add a graphic or diagram incorporate a practice quiz or game.

Use media strategically

Some instructors fall into the trap of media overload. The students may be studying Shakespeare's Hamlet, so they put up links to a hundred different video clips of Shakespearean plays. Yes, one or two are great but, after a while, the overload can be distracting.

As you select media, put it in a location where the student needs to pause to reflect on content or relate to it in a new way. You can also sequence the media so that it occurs when students may be starting to get bored or losing their focus. Media can help you refocus the students.

Diagnostic and developmental/remedial content

With Moodle you can design your course so that it builds in material to help students who may need more time, help, and practice on certain aspects of the Lessons. This is where adaptive learning kicks in and, with Moodle 3.0, you can set links so that, if students do not perform on a specific assessment, they receive a link to return to the instructional content that pertains to the material and also to questions that relate to their current level or competency.

For example, you can build in *Test Yourself!* diagnostic quizzes, which can help pinpoint where a student needs to focus more. This sounds a lot like the old pre-test and post-test approach, but the difference is that it occurs within your Lesson and students can stop along the way to get help. For example, an algebra course could include little *spot check* diagnostic quizzes. They could lead to a review section that is not required for the entire class, but that addresses the specific deficits or gaps that the student has demonstrated. Moodle 3.0's adaptive learning capabilities function like a private tutor.

Reward practice

The more the students practice, the more likely they are to feel good about their ability to perform, both in real-life applications as well as in their final assignments or tests. So, be sure to provide many opportunities for students to practice, and also for them to receive feedback, either automated or personalized from you or a peer.

However, be careful that your quizzes and practice activities are similar in structure, content, and feel to their "high stakes" assignments. If they are not, the students will be discouraged. Also, be sure that the questions and the levels are the same as in the graded assignments. Don't make the final quiz too hard or too easy. Align content, levels of difficulty, time limitations, and testing conditions to those the students will experience later.

Build confidence for final graded performance

All the content and the activities in your Lesson should build toward the students' final performance, whether a final essay, test, or presentation. By the time they reach the end of the Lesson, the students should know what to expect and feel comfortable about what lies ahead. Furthermore, they should have a good idea of where to go when they feel lost or have questions. For example, they may be able to refer to a repository of supplemental readings or solved problems or they can ask questions in the discussion board. At any rate, they should always feel as though there is a supportive presence, either in the course itself or in access to the instructor and fellow students.

Getting started – a simple example

The following screenshot shows a very basic instructional Lesson in Moodle. Note that it is essentially a website and it contains text, links, and an embedded graphic. In fact, it is written in HTML.

Relationship Between Distance and Perspective

In some photographs, space can appear compressed, so that objects appear closer together than they really are. In another photograph of the same scene, space can appear expanded so that objects appear farther apart than they are.

Distance from Camera Determines Perspective

Distortions in perspective are actually caused by the distance of the subject from the camera. The farther a scene is from the camera, the closer the objects in that scene appear. The closer a scene is to the camera, the farther apart objects in that scene appear. Distance compresses the space in a picture, and closeness expands the space.

In the photo below, look at the distance between the columns. The columns closer to the camera appear to be further apart, while those farther from the camera appear closer together.

Photo by Smiles for the world / Alex Lapuerta

Focal Length Does Not Determine Perspective

Many people think these distortions in perspective are caused the focal length of the lens being used. For example, they think that a long lens--a telephoto lens--compresses space, and a short lens--a wide angle lens--expands space. This isn't true.

A telephoto lens enables you to shoot a scene that is farther from the camera. Because the scene is far from the camera, its perspective is compressed. But it is the distance from the camera, not the telephoto lens, that is causing the compression.

A wide angle lens enables you to shoot a scene that is closer to the camera. Because the scene is close to the camera, its perspective is opened. But it is the closeness to the camera, not the wide angle lens, that is causing the opening of the space.

Click the Continue button below to go to the next page in this lesson.

Continue

It is a brief Lesson and so does not have a large number of components. Essentially, the Lesson is introducing a concept (the relationship between distance and perspective). The instruction involves testing the student's knowledge by using a "jump question". If you get it right, you proceed to the next item and, if you get it wrong, you're either taken back to the instructional page or jump to a remedial page. However, the jump question could just as easily ask a student what they are interested in learning next or some other exploratory question.

When the student clicks on the **Continue** button at the bottom of the Lesson page, they are taken to a question page, as shown next:

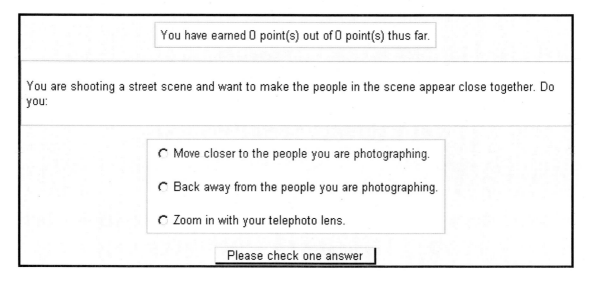

Each answer displays different feedback.

If the student answers correctly, they are taken to the next instructional page. An incorrect answer takes the student to a remedial page.

Remedial: Compressing Perspective

In the photo below, the space between each of the marchers in the front row is the same:

Photo by Celeste Hutchins.

Look at the two men closest to you. You can see that the space between them is over four feet. If one of them reached out his arm, he could not touch the other:

This is the normal sequence for a Lesson in Moodle. Later, we'll discuss how we can make the best use of the Lesson module.

Moodling through a course

Moodle enables students to view resources and complete the activities in any order. For the period the resources and activities are available to the student, the student can access them at any time and in any order. A paragraph from `https://moodle.com/` explains its approach towards e-learning:

> *The word Moodle was originally an acronym for Modular Object-Oriented Dynamic Learning Environment, which is mostly useful to programmers and education theorists. It's also a verb that describes the process of lazily meandering through something, doing things as it occurs, an enjoyable tinkering that often leads to insight and creativity. As such it applies both to the way Moodle was developed, and to the way a student or teacher might approach studying or teaching an online course.*

For our purposes, it's really best to look at the object-oriented approach of Moodle in an instructional sense. If one of your quizzes is not working well, just replace it. You don't have to rewrite the whole Lesson. Instead, you can simply take out the piece and replace it with another. The same applies to the lectures and readings. Is the reading suddenly out of date? No problem. Just replace it with a more up-to-date reading.

Moodle 3.0 is flexible and allows the incorporation of cloud-hosted content, including social media. Replacing and updating readings, videos, and other content is easy. For example, you can add a content page that includes articles that provide relevant content. In the case of a course in tourism, it could be useful to include an article that discusses drones being used to monitor and protect endangered sea turtles in the Pacific coast of Mexico.

First, add the links and size the photo. You can either use a link or upload your file.

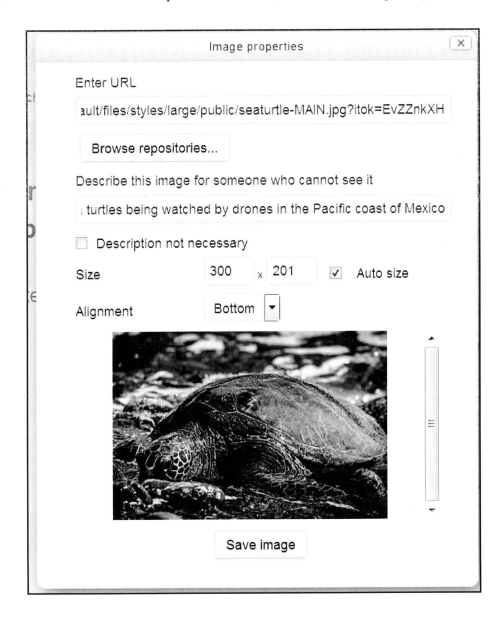

Then review how it looks on your content page. You may find that you need to add more descriptions of the article and also to relate it to the course or unit learning objectives.

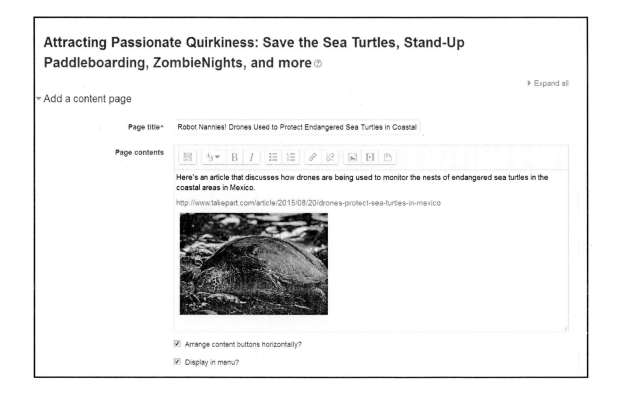

The need for sequential activities

We don't want our students to meander or wander through course items. We want to enforce a specific order of resources and activities. One of the most-requested features in Moodle is the ability to require students to complete their activities in a given sequence.

In Moodle 3.0, you can do this in two different ways. The first involves **Flow control**. You can make sure that your students follow the Lesson path after every correct answer or completed activity. This is done in **Edit settings** under the link **Flow control**:

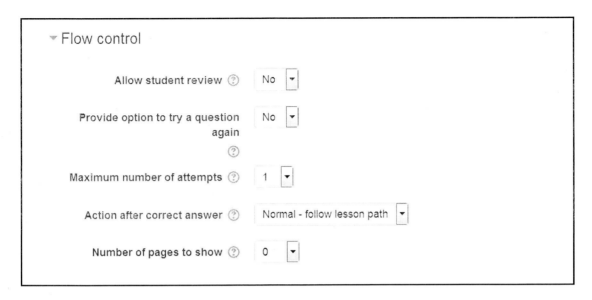

The other approach is to restrict access and allow progress only when a mastery-level grade is achieved. You can start by adding a restriction:

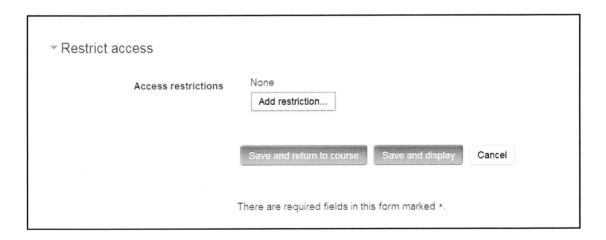

When you click on **Add restriction...**, a window opens and you can restrict access by means of **Grade**, **Group**, **Date** and so on:

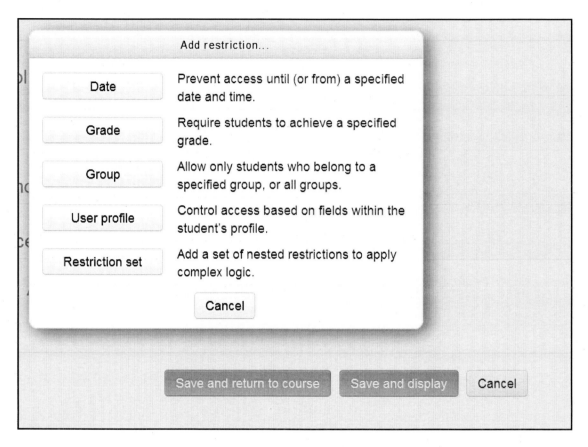

You can then set the grade that the student must achieve before they can move ahead.

Lesson settings

In this section, we will go through the **Editing Lesson** page from top to bottom. We will discuss most of the settings and focus on the ones that are most useful for creating the effect of a deck of flash cards. So, by the end of this section, you will understand how most of the settings on the **Editing Lesson** page affect the student's experience. In later sections, we will discuss how to use these settings to create specific kinds of experiences.

General settings

At the bottom of each question page in a Lesson, you can place a quiz question. **Maximum number of answers** determines the maximum number of answers that each question can have. If each answer sends the student to a different page, then the number of answers is also the number of branches possible. For a flash card experience, you will probably use True/False questions and set this to **2**. After creating question pages, you can increase or decrease this setting without affecting the questions that you have already created. This is shown in the following screenshot:

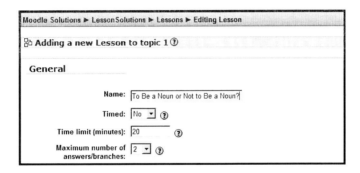

Grade options

If a lesson is only being used for practice, most of the grade options are irrelevant.

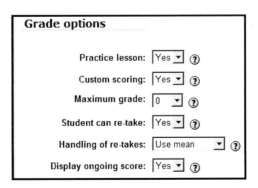

As shown in the previous screenshot, if you set **Practice lesson** to **Yes**, this Lesson will not show up in the **Gradebook**. And if you set **Maximum grade** to 0, the Lesson does not appear in any of the Grades pages. Either way, the student's score in this Lesson will not affect their final grade in the course.

Flow control

Some of the options under **Flow control** make the Lesson behave more like a flash card deck. The other options become irrelevant when a Lesson is used for flash cards.

▼ Flow control

Allow student review ⑦	No ▾
Provide option to try a question again ⑦	Yes ▾
Maximum number of attempts ⑦	2 ▾
Action after correct answer ⑦	Normal - follow lesson path ▾
	Normal - follow lesson path
	Show an unseen page
Number of pages to show ⑦	Show an unanswered page

Allow student review: enables a student to go backwards in a Lesson and retry questions that they got wrong.

Look at the setting for **Action after correct answer**. Note that, in this case, it is set to **Show an unanswered Page**. This means that, after a student answers a question correctly, Moodle will display a page that the student either hasn't seen or that they answered incorrectly. The **Show an unanswered page** setting is usually used during a flash card lesson, to give the student a second chance at answering questions correctly. During a normal Lesson, you will usually use **Allow student review** to enable students to go back to the questions they got wrong.

Display review button displays a button after the student incorrectly answers a question. The button allows the student to re-attempt the question. If your questions have only two answers (true/false, yes/no), then allowing the student to retry a question immediately after getting it wrong doesn't make much sense. It would be more productive to jump to a page explaining why the answer is wrong and use the **Show an unanswered page** setting to give the student another chance at the question, at a later time.

Maximum number of attempts determines how many times a student can attempt any question. It applies to all questions in the Lesson.

Minimum number of questions sets the lower limit for the number of questions used to calculate a student's grade on the Lesson. It is relevant only when the Lesson is going to be graded.

Number of pages to show determines how many pages are shown. If the Lesson contains more than this number, the Lesson ends after reaching the number set here. If the Lesson contains fewer pages than this number, the Lesson ends after every card has been shown. If you set this to 0, the Lesson ends when all cards have been shown.

Lesson formatting

The settings under **Lesson formatting** are used to turn the Lesson into a slide show, which appears in a pop-up window. The **Slide Show** setting creates the slide show window. **Slide show width**, **Slide show height**, and **Slide show background color** set the format of the slide show.

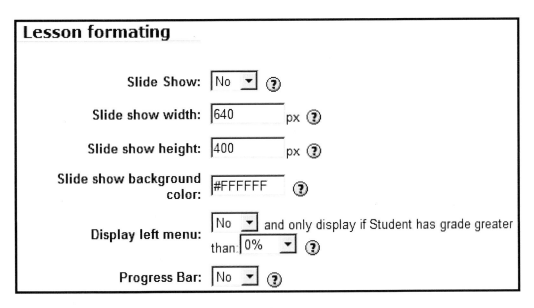

Display left menu displays a navigation bar on the left side of the slide show window. The navigation bar enables the student to navigate to any slide. Without that navigation bar, the student must proceed through the slide show in the order that Moodle displays the Lesson pages and must complete the Lesson to exit (or the student can force the window to close). Sometimes, you want a student to complete the entire Lesson in order, before allowing them to move freely around the Lesson. The setting for **and only display if Student has grade greater than** accomplishes this. Only if the student achieved the specified grade, will they see the navigation menu. You can use this setting to ensure that the student goes completely through the Lesson the first time, before allowing the student to freely move around the Lesson. The **Progress Bar** setting displays a progress bar at the bottom of the Lesson.

Access control

Recall at the beginning of the chapter when we learned that Lessons are the only activity that can be made dependent on completing another activity? This means you can require that the student completes a specific Lesson in your course before allowing the student to access the current Lesson. Now, look at the **Dependent on** setting in the following screenshot:

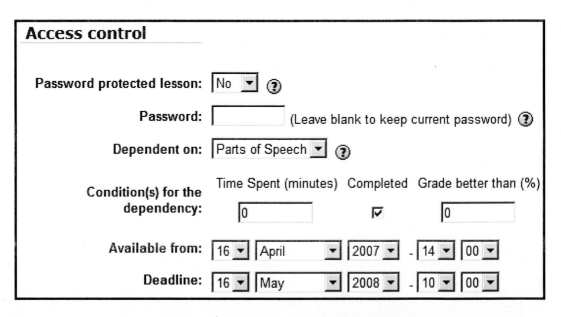

Before the student can access this Lesson, they will need to complete the Lesson **Parts of Speech**. As of now, in Moodle's standard distribution, this is the only kind of activity that supports this type of activity locking.

Other Lesson settings

The **Other** settings area has some settings that can make the Lesson more interesting for the student.

Other	
Link to an activity:	Find the Noun ▼ ⑦
Pop-up to file or web page:	Choose or upload a file ... ⑦
	Show close button: No ▼ - Window height: 100 px, width: 650 px
Display high scores:	No ▼ ⑦
Number of high scores displayed:	10 ⑦
Use this lesson's settings as defaults:	No ▼ ⑦
Visible:	Show ▼

Notice in the previous screenshot, **Link to an activity** is set to **Find the Noun**. This setting places a link on the last page of the Lesson to the activity or resource specified. The drop-down list contains all of the resources and activities in the current course. The user must click the link to be taken to the location. So this setting doesn't force the user to proceed to a specific place after the Lesson.

The **Choose or upload a file...** setting enables you to specify a file that is displayed in a separate window at the beginning of the Lesson. This can be useful if you want the student to refer to something during the Lesson. For example, you could display a diagram and present a series of Lesson pages that refer to that diagram. Be careful about combining this with the **Slide Show** setting under Lesson formatting. If you use them both, you'll have Moodle displayed in one window, the file displayed in another, and the slide show Lesson displayed in a third window.

Display high scores lets the high-scoring students choose a name to post their scores under. This setting doesn't do anything if you make the Lesson a **Practice lesson**.

Controlling the flow through a Lesson

If your Lesson questions have all true/false or yes/no answers, you will probably set **Maximum number of answers** to **2**. If you use more than two answers per question, consider whether you want to create a jump page for each answer. If you create a unique jump page for every answer on the question pages and you use three answers per question, how many cards will there be in your flash card deck? The answer is your Lesson will have three pages for each flash card, the card itself, plus two jump pages for remedial information.

We don't want to spend all day creating a short Lesson, but we still want to show remedial information when a student selects the wrong answer. Consider phrasing your questions, answers, and remedial pages so that one remedial page can cover all of the incorrect responses. This sort of flow will help you reduce the number of remedial pages that have to be created.

If you must give different feedback for each answer to a question, consider using a quiz instead of a Lesson. In Chapter 4, *Assessment*, the *Adding feedback to quiz questions* section shows you how to create feedback for each individual answer in a quiz question. While a remedial page in a Lesson can consist of anything that you can put on a web page, feedback can only consist of text. However, quizzes are usually easier to create than Lessons. If a quiz with feedback will suffice, you can probably create it faster than the branching Lesson. But, if your feedback must be feature rich, there's nothing better than Moodle's Lesson module.

Further, in Moodle 3.0, you can link to cloud-based resources and include additional content pages that will help students master the content so that they can perform well and demonstrate their knowledge and/or skills.

Use a Lesson to create a deck of flash cards

Flash cards are a classic teaching strategy. In addition to a learning experience, flash cards also make a good self-assessment tool for students. You can use a Lesson, as if it's an online deck of flash cards. One advantage of using an online system is that log files tell you whether a student completed the flash card activity and how well the student did.

Keep it moving

Students are accustomed to a flash card activity moving quickly. Showing a remedial page after each incorrect response will slow down the activity. Consider using only question feedback, without remedial pages in between cards.

In a flash card lesson, every page will be a question page. In a Lesson, a question page can have any content that you can put on a normal web page. So, each page in your flash card lesson can consist of a fully featured web page, with a question at the bottom and some text-only feedback for each answer.

When setting the jumps for each answer on the question page (on the card), make sure that a correct answer takes the student to the next page and an incorrect answer keeps them on the same page. Again, this duplicates our physical experience with flash cards. When we get the correct answer, we move on to the next card. When we get the wrong answer, we try again until we've got it right.

Lesson settings that help create a flash card experience

For a flash card lesson, you will probably set **Practice lesson** to **Yes** so that the grade for this Lesson will not show up in the **Gradebook**. As stated previously, setting **Maximum grade** to 0 will prevent this activity from showing up in the **Gradebook**. However, it will also prevent a student from seeing their score on the activity. If you want the student to see how well they did on the Lesson, set **Practice lesson** to **Yes** and use a maximum grade that makes sense, such as one point per correct answer.

Allow student review enables a student to go backwards in a Lesson and retry questions that they got wrong. In a flash card activity, this is usually set to **No**. Instead, we usually set **Action after correct answer** to **Show an unanswered page**. That means after a student answers a flash card question incorrectly, Moodle might display that card again during the same session. If the student answers the question correctly, that card is not shown again during the same session. This is how most of us are accustomed to using physical flash cards.

Number of pages (cards) to show determines how many pages are shown. You usually want a flash card session to be short. If the Lesson contains more than this number, the Lesson ends after reaching the number set here. If the Lesson contains fewer than this number, the Lesson ends after every card has been shown. For a flash card lesson, set this to less than the total number of cards.

You can use the **Slide Show** setting to display the Lesson in a separate window and make that window the size of a flash card. This can help create the effect of a deck of cards.

When the student uses a physical deck of flash cards, they can see approximately how far into the deck they are. The **Progress bar** setting can help to create this effect with your online deck of flash cards.

Use an ungraded Lesson to generate materials and strategies for real-world applications

You may consider Moodle as a platform for schools, colleges, or universities. But, it's often a very good place to bring together teams in a business, not-for-profit organization, or small enterprise. For example, let's think of the case of a group that has come together for the promotion of tourism. It's easy to create a Lesson that directs learners through different activities so that, at the end of the course, they've learned how to research their potential market and have developed a marketing plan for promoting their town, community, or specific historical or natural resource.

For example, in this course, one of the learning objectives is to identify activities that could attract unique groups of tourists, especially those who are passionate and loyal. So we can set up content pages that allow students to move through them.

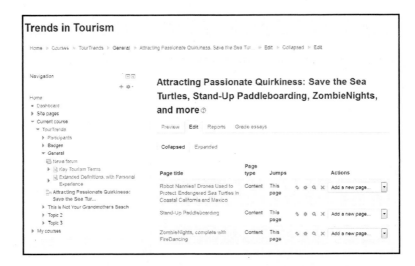

As we add the page, we can also make sure that we automatically guide the student through the material by incorporating the jumps.

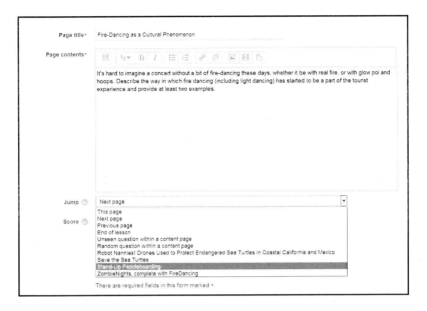

Keep in mind that, with Moodle 3.0, if you're adding a video, you can either embed the code using HTML or simply put a link in the video icon and Moodle's player will play the video.

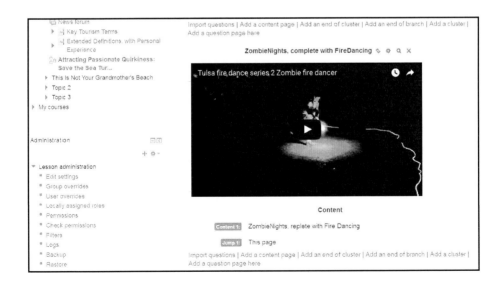

Use an ungraded Lesson to step through instructions

This is a good time to implement a concept called **precorrection.** Briefly, precorrection is anticipating mistakes that students might make and providing instruction to help them avoid those mistakes. Consider, you give a complex assignment to students. You know that even if you supply them with written instructions, they are likely to make mistakes, even when following the instructions. You might also give the students a video demo and a *Frequently Made Mistakes* document. You could even host a chat before the assignment to answer any questions they have about how to complete it. If you focus these items on the parts of the assignment that are most likely to cause trouble, they become examples of precorrection.

You can use a Lesson to give students precorrection for difficult instructions. Place directions that should be read in a specific order on a series of Lesson pages. See to it that the students step through those pages. This has several advantages over placing all of the instructions on one page. They are as follows:

- Moodle will log the students' view of the Lesson pages so that you can confirm they have read the instructions.
- While the length of a Lesson page is unlimited, the tendency when creating them is to keep them short. This encourages you to break up the directions into smaller chunks, which are easier for students to understand.
- You can insert a question page after each step, to confirm the user's understanding of the step. Question feedback and remedial pages can correct the students' understanding, before they move to the next step.

If you use this technique, the Lesson should probably be a **Practice lesson** so that the student's grade doesn't affect their final grade for the course.

A workaround

Lessons are designed to primarily be a teaching tool and only secondarily an assessment tool. However, if you decide that you prefer to use a Lesson for assessment, you can work around this limitation. This workaround enables you to determine whether a student answered incorrectly on an initial question or on a remedial question. A low score on remedial questions should prompt action on the teacher's part such as contacting the student and offering additional help.

Let's start by creating a question page:

Now, let's start to populate the questions with answers. Notice that we're adding **Jump** directions so that, as the students select certain answers, they'll go to different places in the course. If they need more review, the **Jump** can take them to a review page. Or, if they've mastered the topic, they can move on:

You have seen how a Lesson usually consists of an instructional page followed by a question page and that, when a student answers a question incorrectly, the Lesson can display a response and it can also direct them back to a remedial page. You can do that by incorporating a **Jump** link.

Also, a correct response takes the individual directly to a different page.

If you do not want to return to the original content page, you can link to a new content page, which would be a *remedial* page. Then, after the remedial page, you can present another question on the same topic. Now, imagine a Lesson that covers three items. Each item has its own instructional page followed by a question page and a remedial page followed by another question page. So, not counting the entry and exit pages, there would be:

- Three topic pages (content pages)
- Three question pages
- Three remedial topic pages (content pages)
- Three remedial question pages

If you were looking at the **Gradebook** for this Lesson and a student's grade indicated that they got two questions wrong, you could determine whether it was because they gave:

- One incorrect response on two of the items
- Two incorrect responses for the same item

If the student answered incorrectly on both the first and the remedial questions for the same item, it could indicate the student is having trouble with that item. But the **Gradebook** won't tell you that. You will need to drill down from the **Gradebook** into the Lesson to see that student's score for each question. From the **Gradebook**, you would select the category in which the Lesson is placed.

The following screenshot illustrates how you can take a look at the performance of the students in the course. Knowing what the students are thinking and selecting can help you gain an overall understanding of where your students are in terms of achieving learning objectives.

Multichoice - Multiple-answer: Save the Sea Turtles	Class statistics
Question: Review your knowledge of tourism focused on saving sea turtles. Which items relate to sea turtle eco-tourism?	
Answer:	
☐ Robotic drones are used to monitor nesting areas.	No one checked this.
☐ Stand Up Paddleboarding competitions attract tourists to beach towns such as Sayulita in Mexico.	No one checked this.
☐ Festivals where people dress up like zombies and play are popular. They often include firedancing.	No one checked this.
☐ All of the above	No one checked this.

Summary

Lessons are a flexible tool for creating both instructional and assessment experiences. The key to making the best use of them is planning. When creating a Lesson, plan the flow within the lesson. Know which jumps you want to make before you start creating the Lesson and plan how you want to combine the Lesson with other activities into a larger flow. For example, many users favor a flow that puts a non-interactive, reading or viewing activity first, then an interactive Lesson, followed by a quiz, and finally a chat or forum for review.

Since a Lesson offers both presentation and question capabilities, it is tempting to try to make it do the work of both a web page and a quiz. However, a Lesson functions best when used as a bridge between those two resources. Don't be afraid to experiment with using Lessons in new ways. Let us know about your experiences on the official `https://moodle.org/` user forums.

6
Wiki Solutions

A wiki can be one of the most flexible collaborative tools one has in the e-learning toolkit. While you may think of a wiki as a place to jointly contribute information in collaborative encyclopedia-like articles (as in the case of Wikipedia), you'll find that in Moodle, a wiki opens up a wide range of collaborative possibilities, that allow people to learn from each other and boost motivation at the same time. You can even use a wiki for group projects and presentations. In addition, a wiki can be used to develop customized, individualized learning modules to employ what is often referred to as **differential learning**. With individual wikis, you can differentiate the learning experience for your students. In this chapter, you will learn how to create group wikis for group and team collaborations, as well as how to develop individualized learning spaces with individual wikis. One of the benefits of individualized learning in wikis is that, if your students need either remediation or enrichment, you can provide it to them. You can also accommodate differences in learning styles and preferences by incorporating multimedia.

Using wikis to achieve learning objectives

In this section, we will discuss the importance of using the course outcomes and learning objectives to make decisions about course content, delivery mode, and instructional strategy. Course outcomes and unit-level learning objectives help arrange a course by giving it a theme. As a useful organizing tool, a learning objective must not only be specific but also broad enough to apply to a variety of topics. Learning objectives generally encompass the big ideas in the course. Keep in mind that an idea is not necessarily a big idea. A big idea must enable the student to organize information and find relationships among the information learned during a course. At its best, a big idea also helps the student to relate what is learned in the course to his/her own life. For example, a *big idea* in a course called Survey of American Literature could be described by this question: What does it mean to be an American? Then, the wiki could use examples from different works of

American literature to illustrate what it means to be an American, and also how the concept evolved over time.

This process of organizing information around a big idea and relating it to other information and one's life, requires thought and effort from the student. A class wiki can be a good tool for recording these thoughts.

During the course, students can use a wiki to relate new knowledge back to the big ideas. So, set aside a wiki for the big ideas and prepopulate it with them. If there are several big ideas, consider creating an initial page for each big idea. Then, as each topic is covered, ask the students to add to the wiki beneath the appropriate big idea(s). The additions should relate the acquired knowledge back to the big idea. So, in the example of the Survey of American Literature, individuals could select examples from the literature they are reading to show how they illustrate what it means to be an American at certain points in time and among specific groups. Then, students could then relate it to their own experiences and perceptions. It would be possible as well to ask students to look at the various ideas from different vantage points. For example, what would it mean to be a woman in Edith Wharton's New York City? Or, what would it mean to be a member of the Cherokee Nation during the time of the Trail of Tears?

We are assuming that the *big idea wiki* will be open to the entire class. That will make it a collaborative project. If you prefer, you can keep this activity private between the individual and the teacher. Both strategies can be very useful and result in a building block approach to knowledge, which also allows one to show the development of different perspectives.

Why a wiki?

Moodle offers several tools that students can use for a repeated writing assignment, with instructor feedback. Forums and blogs are also good options. So, why use a wiki? In this section, we will explore the reasons to use a wiki for relating course material back to the big ideas. Our primary goal isn't to convince you that this is the only way, but to present you with all the factors you need to make a good decision for your course and your students. If we arrive at different conclusions, that's fine.

Wiki versus forum

For integrating knowledge into a big idea, wikis have several advantages over forums as explained next:

- The first advantage applies only if you want the big idea wiki to be an individual activity. In Moodle 3.0, it is possible for an entire class to work on a document together so that what they develop is a joint product. Or, each student can have his or her own wiki. They can then work on it alone, with the instructor or with their classmates.

- Everyone who uses the forum can see all the postings, even if they can't edit them. You may set up individual wikis by creating a forum with the **Group mode** set to **Separategroups**. This will limit the use of the forum to just the individual student and the teacher. However, forums are not meant to be a place where just one individual records his/her thoughts and just one individual responds (you or the teacher). If you want each student to think and record his/her thoughts independently, a forum might not be the best choice.

- Second, remember that one of the purposes of using a big idea is to provide a unifying theme for course material. If you devote a forum topic to one big idea, then at the end of the course you will have a collection of forum postings about that big idea. But if you create a wiki page for a big idea, then at the end of the course you have a single document devoted to that big idea. I feel that a wiki's structure does more to encourage the production of unified knowledge than a forum does. For example, one of your students' most popular online resources will be `https://www.wikipedia.org/`.

- Third, your students' understanding of how new knowledge relates to the big idea can change drastically during a course. A wiki enables and encourages repeated editing of an entry. The entry grows and changes as the student's understanding changes. In a forum, the student would need to create a new reply each time his/her understanding changes. A forum offers a good history of the student's changing understanding. However, the wiki's format does a better job in presenting the current state of your students' understanding.

Wiki versus blog

In Moodle, each student can have a blog. This is turned on by default. However, a student's blog is not attached to any course; that is, you do not access a Moodle blog by going into a course and selecting the blog. Each student has his or her own blog. Instead, you view the user's profile and access that user's blog from there. In Moodle 3.0 you can now associate blog entries with a current course. However, the blogs can be seen in other parts of Moodle, so it could be a rather messy and unfocused process.

If your administrator allows it, you can register external blogs such as WordPress and Blogger. In this case, the blog posts from WordPress and Blogger would automatically go into the Moodle blog. While this might seem like a good idea, the automatic feed can result in a very messy and unfocused set of blog posts within your course. It is almost impossible to keep it as focused as in a wiki.

In addition, a wiki allows you to provide excellent and focused feedback on their post, which could be writing or embedded multimedia. For these reasons, a Moodle blog is probably not the best way to have students relate new material to big ideas.

An assignment

Before Moodle 3.0, there was an activity entitled **journal**, which was a bit like Notes. In newer versions of Moodle, online text assignment is intended to replace the journal activity. It also shares the journal's disadvantages of not saving a history of the student's edits and forcing you to make the activity individual. However, an assignment does enable you to use any one of Moodle's standard or custom grading scales to grade the student's assignment and to leave a written feedback.

Let's agree to disagree

We examined five activities for making big ideas as a part of our course. While you might disagree with my conclusion (I assume about four-fifths of my readers will), we are glad that you stuck with the arguments this far. If you have reached a different conclusion, it is implied that you did so in a logical, informed way. The table that's coming up compares each of the options we looked at:

Activity	Saves history	Enables grading	Enables feedback	Enables collaboration	Individual activity	Exists within course
Assignment	No	Yes	Yes	Yes	Yes	Yes
Blog	Yes	No	No	No	Yes	No
Forum	Yes	Yes	Yes	Yes	Yes	Yes
Journal	No	Yes	Yes	No	Yes	Contributed plugin
Wiki	Yes	No	Yes	Yes	Yes	Yes

There is no perfect option here. We would suggest you use an online text assignment after each topic and require the student to relate material learned in that topic to the big ideas of the course. At the end of the course, you could require the student to copy and paste all of the topic assignments into one last assignment and revise them into a final big idea submission. There is much discussion about the appropriate and creative uses of these activities on the Moodle forums.

Individual student wikis

We usually think of a wiki as a group activity. However, Moodle enables you to create an individual wiki for each student enrolled in your course. Every student gets his/her own wiki, which only you and the student can edit. Like any other activity, you can choose whether to allow other students and groups to see each other's wikis.

This doesn't mean that you must create each student's wiki one at a time. Instead, you could create a wiki as you normally would and designate it as a *Student Wiki*. The first time that any student accesses the wiki, Moodle creates that student's personal wiki.

Individual student wikis can be used for several teaching strategies. In this section, we'll explore two of them: one-on-one instruction and guided note taking.

In earlier chapters, we discussed the process by which individuals learn in a group setting. One way is through social learning. Keep in mind that social learning can take place with several people or it can work with a one-to-one communication with the instructor. You can hold one-to-one, online discussions with your students by giving each of them an individual wiki. If you set the **Group mode** to **No**, your discussions can be kept private.

Using a wiki for these discussions enables students to review and edit previous posts as their understanding changes. It also puts all the discussion in one place, unlike using a series of e-mail messages or forum postings.

It also allows students to incorporate their social media sites and posts without having to establish a feed. For example, a student can incorporate a post in Tumblr or A photo from Flickr by embedding the HTML or simply including a link.

Sometimes it is better to upload a graphic or a media file directly to Moodle, but in many cases the file size is too large and puts too much pressure on the server, and so it is best to incorporate an embedded link or player, especially in the case of video or audio. In that case, it is a good idea to use reliable and well-known providers, such as YouTube and SoundCloud.

Creating individual wikis

This book assumes some proficiency with Moodle, so I won't give click-by-click directions for creating a wiki. In Moodle 3.0, you select the **Wiki** activity from the same menu as the other activities:

The key to creating an individual wiki for each student is the **Wiki mode** setting on the **Editing Wiki** page. From the **Wiki mode** drop-down menu, select **Individual wiki**. This is shown in the following screenshot:

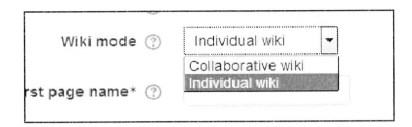

Each time a new student accesses the wiki from the course home page, an individual wiki will be created for that student. The second and subsequent times a student accesses the wiki, he/she is taken to that student's personal wiki.

Active reading strategies with individual student wikis

Earlier chapters discuss the importance of interacting with the course content and concepts and of practicing as much as possible. Practice can mean working through quizzes. It can also mean note-taking as a way to practice *active reading* and to avoid passivity. In this case, wikis can be used for making guided notes. In a traditional classroom, you might copy a high-level outline for the course and distribute it to the students. They could use this as a guide for taking notes. In an online course, you can create a wiki for each student to populate with course notes. This wiki can have starting pages, which provide a guide for the student to enter notes. In this section, we'll see how to create an individual wiki for each student in a course and how to prepopulate that wiki with starting pages that you create. This gives each student a place for guided note taking. **Guided note-taking** can be used effectively with the following instructional content to make sure that students actively engage with the material and that connections are being made between the course content, the course outcomes, and the activities.

Active reading/viewing are ideal for courses with the following elements:

- Text/readings
- Multimedia presentations
- Videos
- Audio lectures, debates, interviews, and stories

To ensure a positive learning experience while students are taking notes, it is a good idea to create a template that helps them structure the information and keep connected to the course outcomes.

Be sure to relate each piece of course content (reading, video, and so on) to the learning objective or course outcome it corresponds to and state that explicitly at the top of the particular wiki that will connect to it.

Also, be sure to remind students of the kinds of assessment that they will need to do to demonstrate learning. If they are to complete a quiz at the end of the course, be sure to indicate where and how, and to help students focus their note-taking toward the end goal, their assessment event. You may also wish to include links to specific outside resources and reference them to the specific sections in their texts. In this case, using the Book function makes it possible to have a self-contained and manageable connection between the wiki's exploratory/investigative/collaborative focus and the actual knowledge or skill item addressed in the learning objective.

Detailed directions to create an individual wiki are in the subsections that follow. The overall process follows this order:

1. **Create the Wiki's starting pages**: Create a text file for the wiki's homepage. If desired, create additional text files for additional starting pages. Upload text files to the course.
2. **Create the individual student Wiki**: Create an individual student wiki in your course. While creating the wiki, select the text files for the initial pages. Test the wiki as a student.

Creating a text file for the wiki's starting page

For every starting page that you want your wiki to have, you must create a new page. You can then populate it by copying and pasting content or you can upload a text file.

Text files use Wiki Markup for formatting commands. The purpose of these commands is to enable an author to quickly format text while typing, without going to a menu. For example, to create a small headline (the equivalent of a Heading 3 in Word or your HTML editor), you would type `!Headline`.

To create a medium headline (Heading 2), use two exclamation marks. For a large headline (Heading 1), use three exclamation marks. For example, to create a medium headline (the equivalent of a Heading 2 in Word or your HTML editor), you would type `!!Headline`.

If you want the starting page of your wiki to contain the first-level headings for an outline, you might create a text file called `Microscopy` that contains this text:

```
!!!Microscopy and Specimen Preparation
[Lenses and the Bending of Light | Lenses_and_the_Bending_of_Light]
[The Light Microscope | The_Light_Microscope]
[Preparation and Staining of Specimens |
Preparation_and_Staining_of_Specimens]
```

If you chose that text file as the starting page for a wiki, the first time a student accessed the wiki he/she would see the following:

Note that the name of the text file, **Microscopy**, became the name of the page. Also note that the text preceded by ! ! ! became a top-level heading and the text inside square brackets became links.

At this page, the student would then select the **Edit** link and begin filling in this outline.

Building on our previous example, you can enter second level headings on the same page. The `Microscopy.txt` file would contain this:

```
!!!Microscopy and Specimen Preparation

!!Lenses and the Bending of Light

!Refraction

!Focal Point

!!The Light Microscope
!The Bright-field Microscope

!Resolution

!The Dark-field Microscope

!!Preparation and Staining of Specimens

!Fixation

!Dyes and Simple Staining

!Differential Staining
```

When that text file is uploaded and made a starting page for the wiki.

If you leave this page as it is, the student might put all of his/her notes for these topics on this one page. If you want to guide the student into using separate pages for each of these topics, you will need to create a separate page for each topic. You can put links to the topic pages from this starting page. It is the same idea as creating a homepage and providing links to the inside pages of a website.

Creating multiple starting pages

In the previous section, you saw how to create a single starting page for a wiki. You can also create multiple starting pages for a wiki and link to those pages from the wiki's homepage.

In our example, we want to create four pages for our wiki:

- The Starting Page
- Lenses and the Bending of Light
- The Light Microscope
- Preparation and Staining of Specimens

On the starting page, we want links to the other three pages.

First, let's discuss how to create multiple starting pages. We will then discuss how to create links to the starting pages from the wiki's homepage.

Multiple text files create multiple starting pages

So, we need to create and upload a text file for each starting page in our wiki. In our example, the text files for the starting page and the three topic pages would look like this:

```
Microscopy.txt
!!!Microscopy and Specimen Preparation
[Lenses and the Bending of Light | Lenses_and_the_Bending_of_Light]
[The Light Microscope | The_Light_Microscope]
[Preparation and Staining of Specimens |
Preparation_and_Staining_of_Specimens]
Lenses_and_the_Bending_of_Light.txt
!!Lenses and the Bending of Light
!Refraction
!Focal Point
The_Light_Microscope.txt
!!The Light Microscope
!The Bright-field Microscope
!Resolution
!The Dark-field Microscope
```

```
Preparation_and_Staining_of_Specimens.txt
!!Preparation and Staining of Specimens
!Fixation
!Dyes and Simple Staining

!Differential Staining
```

Creating links to other starting pages

The `Microscopy.txt` file will have links to the other three pages. In the Wiki Markup language, links are enclosed in square brackets, such as `[The_Light_Microscope]` where `The_Light_Microscope` is the name of the page in the wiki. By default, the link displays the name of the page. If you want the link to display something other than the name of the page, such as `Light Microscopes`, you can add that to the markup:

```
[Light Microscopes | The_Light_Microscope]
```

This creates a link that displays **LightMicroscopes** and takes the reader to a page called **The_Light_Microscope**.

In the links, note that the page names have underscores in them. Remember that the first part, `LightMicroscopes`, is what the link will display. The second part, `The_Light_Microscope`, is the page that the link jumps to.

Why the underscores? These underscores are to accommodate a quirk that Moodle has. When Moodle uploads the text files that create these pages, it adds underscores to their names. For example, if you upload a file called `The Light Microscope.txt`, Moodle changes its name to `The_Light_Microscope.txt`. As the wiki pages are named after the text files that you upload, the pages will also have underscores in their names. Therefore, the links to the starting pages created from those text files need the underscores.

After you've created a text file for each starting page that you want in your wiki, you are ready to upload them.

Creating an individual student wiki in your course

Once again, this book assumes some proficiency with Moodle. So we won't provide click-by-click directions for creating a wiki.

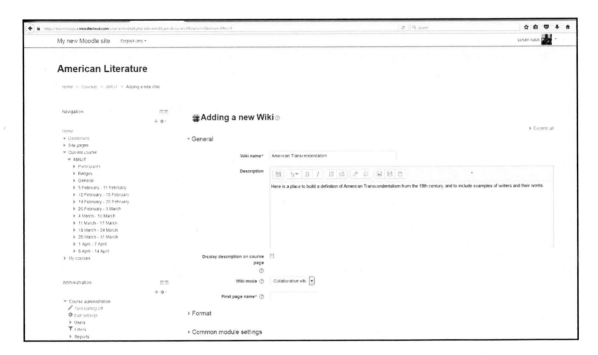

The key is to select **Individual wiki** from the **Wiki mode** drop-down menu while creating the wiki. If you are using an earlier version than Moodle 2.0, the drop-down menu may still say **Student** instead of **Individual**.

In Moodle 3.x , the menu has changed, and the options are **Collaborative wiki** and **Individual wiki**:

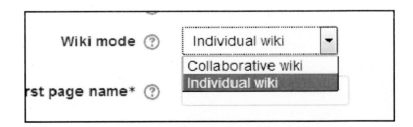

Now each time a new student accesses the wiki from the course home page, an individual wiki will be created for that student. The second and subsequent times a student accesses the wiki, he/she is taken to that student's personal wiki.

The **HTML Mode** setting will affect how your starting page looks. In the following example, I've selected **No HTML** because I am using Wiki Markup language in the text files:

If I select one of the HTML modes, the starting page will not be displayed properly because the text file doesn't contain valid HTML; it contains Wiki Markup instead.

Here is how the Wiki entry would appear using Wiki Markup:

> ## Microscopy
>
> ## Microscopy and Specimen Preparation
>
> <u>Lenses and the Bending of Light</u> The Light Microscope Preparation and Staining of Specimens

You can see that the line breaks between the links were lost. If you want to use HTML in your wiki, the text files that create your initial pages must be written with HTML. If you want to use Wiki Markup language, the text files must be written in Wiki Markup language.

Test the wiki as a student

When creating a course, it is helpful to keep two separate browsers running, such as Internet Explorer and Firefox. In one browser, create the course. In the other, log in as a student and test as you create. If you are not using e-mail or manual-based registration and are using LDAP or an external database for authentication, you may have to talk to the network administrator (or Moodle administrator) to get a student account created.

The result of uploading these text files and choosing **Microscopy** as the starting page looks like the following:

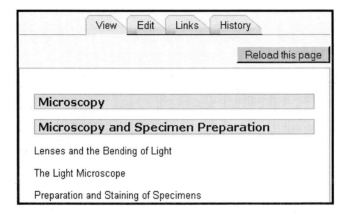

If we select the **Sitemap** for the wiki, you can see the organization of the starting pages in the following screenshot:

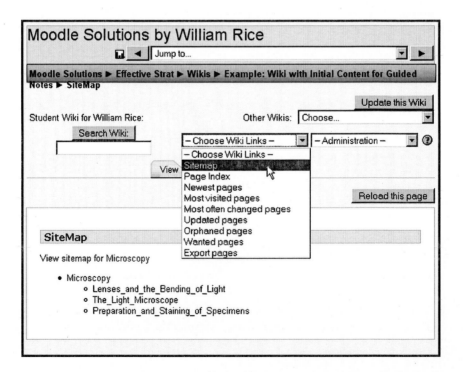

Once a student has viewed the wiki, you can no longer change the starting page(s). At that point, if you want a wiki with different starting pages, you must create a new wiki.

Leveraging guided notes created by students

In the business world, to *leverage* something is to take maximum advantage of it. You can leverage the guided notes created by your students. First, the students' notes tell you what they thought you wanted them to learn and what they considered important. This might be very different from what you actually wanted them to learn, and from what you considered important. Imagine giving your students a test and discovering that the entire class has learned some very different material from what you included in the test. Reviewing the students' guided notes periodically can avoid this kind of surprise and give insight into their progress. This is something we can't do when the students take notes on paper.

Further, you can help them be active learners by helping them internalize the process of making connections between the course content and the learning objectives, and then the final assessment (quiz, and so on) in which they demonstrate the achievement of course outcomes.

Guide them so that active reading/viewing becomes automatic: Read => Reflect (with wiki/guided questions) => Connect (to practice assessment, quiz, essay, and so on).

Then, make students aware of the value of the "active reading" approach. Encourage sharing of individual wikis by creating a discussion thread that gives people access to each other's wikis, if they so choose.

Suggested wiki etiquette

No wiki software offers every feature. Each wiki application offers its own blend of features. Some points of wiki etiquettes apply only to certain features and others only to certain environments. With Moodle's wiki features and the e-learning environment in mind, here are suggested etiquettes for your Moodle wikis.

- **Participate**: Add a paragraph, correct some grammar or some spelling, fix a broken link, create a new page, and so on. A wiki is a collaboration, so jump in and collaborate.
- **Encourage each other**: The wiki is a great place to develop a learning community and a spirit of exploration, debate, and excitement.
- **Learning is a work in progress**: Nothing is set in stone. Be open to out-of-the-box ideas. Keep in mind that everything can be changed and nothing is rigid. Develop

a sense of exploration, rather than of defending your turf.

- **Help to organize and create structure**: Even if you're not creating new content, you can organize the already-existing content. Give some meaningful names to your pages to help users easily identify them. Create cross-links between pages. When you find content on a page that belongs to a different page, cut and paste it. Making information easy to find is just as important as creating it.

- **Comment thoughtfully**: A wiki is not instant messaging. It's not meant to be a high-speed conversation. And while a wiki is not the most formal type of writing, it is not entirely informal. Even if what you write is deleted, it will remain in the wiki's history. Express your opinions carefully.

- **Add items to lists**: If someone has created a list of items, feel free to add to it. But add the items in alphabetical or logical order.

- **Be polite**: Just as with chats, it's easy to misinterpret the tone of a comment. So, be polite.

- **Don't write "click here"**: Instead, create links that describe what the reader will see when they follow the link.

- **Avoid creating blank pages**: Remember that, when you insert a link into a wiki (using Camel Case or square brackets), a page is created when you click on the link, and not otherwise. Unless you have content to add, don't click on a link that creates a new page. All pages show up in the site map, including blank pages. A sitemap full of blank pages can mislead and disappoint the reader. If you have some content for the page, by all means, create it. If not, leave the link untouched.

- **Preserve the meaning**: *The meaning of something can change with its context.* When you move or delete material, make sure that you are not unintentionally changing the meaning of the remaining material.

- **Relax! Don't take it personally**: Your work will be edited, and you will not agree with every change. That's the nature of collaboration.

- **Delete carefully**: If you can achieve your goal by adding to or editing an entry, do that instead of deleting it. Most contributors have reasons for adding an entry. They might feel their time has been wasted if they see their entries being deleted. If you do delete an entry, be sure to send an e-mail or note to the contributor to explain why you did so.

- **Discuss things elsewhere**: Moodle enables you to see who has edited an entry. If you want to discuss an entry with its authors, use means such as e-mail, chats, forums, and so on. The wiki is the place to produce content, not to discuss it.

Summary

In this chapter, we saw how to use a wiki for relating material to a big idea, one-on-one discussion, and guided note-taking. The section on big idea wikis compared Moodle's Wiki module to its Assignment, Blog, Forum, and Notes modules. You may have noticed that, in Moodle, these modules are missing some elements that you would expect, but include some elements that surprise you. This is because each of Module's capabilities and limitations are chosen so that they support online learning and fit into Moodle's environment. For example, Moodle notes do not allow other participants to comment. This is because the developers and community are still discussing whether notes comments will pull valuable discussion out of a blog and into a student's notes (recall that a blog belongs to a user, not to a course). To find out more about the rationale behind decisions like this, and to compare capabilities of the various module's, read the www.moodle.org forums.

The ability to create individual student wikis is one of Moodle's surprising, and often under-used capabilities. The same can be said for creating starting pages in a wiki. Whenever you need to guide a student's writing, consider an individual wiki with starting pages. You can also find other creative uses of Moodle wikis. Keep in mind that a wiki is a great way to guide students in active learning, and to relate content to outcomes, learning objectives, and assessments.

7
Glossary Solutions

Moodle's glossary activity provides the framework for creating and then modifying/maintaining a number of definitions that tie in with the instructional material for the unit. Most people think of glossaries as nothing more than special-purpose, online dictionaries. In Moodle, glossaries can be used in a number of ways, and you can create useful, multi-functional activities that help your students achieve the learning objectives of the course. For example, you can create key concept reviews, a student's directory, and group assignments. You can help students develop a way to organize knowledge and begin to make connections between items and prior knowledge. But a glossary can also be an enjoyable, collaborative activity as well as a teaching tool for your class. Let's look at the capabilities of the Glossary module first, and then ideas for using glossaries for more than just vocabulary building.

Helping students learn – schema building

One of the most exciting uses of the glossary is to help learners develop categories of knowledge, make connections to their experience, and to elaborate the concepts.

For this purpose, glossaries help students create what educational psychologists refer to as a schema (plural is schemata). A schema is a category that represents general knowledge. Think of it as a file folder where you can organize your knowledge. A successful educational project allows learners to create a number of file folders, or schemata. At the end of the day, the resultant structure is an interconnected web of nodes of knowledge, which encourages associations and additional ways of thinking.

So, when creating a glossary, you will be creating a database of individual entries, and will be grouping them by creating labels that you will attach to the schemata.

Once you have developed the structure of your glossaries/schemata, you can then develop activities that foster interactive, collaborative learning. These activities are as follows:

- Identification and definition activities
- Discussing connection to prior knowledge and experience
- Elaborating concepts
- Synthesizing information between categories, and use it to solve problems and address issues

These are just a few ways to use the glossaries for schema building and other learning activities. Be sure to tie in whatever activities you design with the course outcomes and the learning objectives.

Moodle's glossary functions

A practical and easy-to-understand way of engaging your students, and encouraging them to start developing schema in an interactive way, is to create a glossary. In Moodle, a glossary is an activity. To add a glossary, follow these steps:

1. Click on the **Turn editing on** button.
2. Select **Glossary** from the **Add an activity or resource** link.

3. On the **Adding a new Glossary** page, give your new glossary a descriptive name.
4. Describe the purpose of the glossary and provide instructions or background information, links, and so on, in the **Description** area.
5. Complete the **General** and **Grade options** and the **Common module settings**.
6. Click on the **Save and return to course** button at the bottom of the page.

You will be able to add a description of the glossary and its purpose. This is a good place to connect the purpose to the learning objectives of the course.

You can also choose to display the description on the course page, and also make it global. There are two types of glossary: main and secondary. The advantages of a secondary glossary include its increased flexibility and collaborative opportunities.

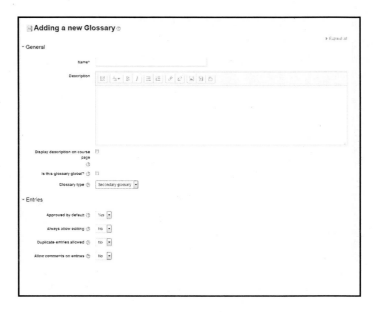

After you create a new glossary, let your students know that they will be organizing their entries alphabetically. The following screenshot shows how an entry for a collaborative glossary for **Coyotes** would appear:

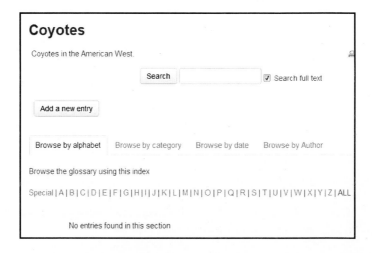

Automatic linking to a glossary

Moodle can automatically link a term, wherever it appears in a course, to the term's glossary entry. Note that the following three things must be set for this to happen:

- The glossary must be in the same course as the term, or the glossary must be available throughout the site (see the next section)
- The term must match the name of the glossary entry or one of the entry's aliases
- Automatic linking must be turned *on* for the glossary and glossary entry

Course versus site glossaries

When you create a glossary, it is added to the course in which you created it. If you have administrator privileges on your Moodle site, you can make a glossary global, which makes it active for every course on your site.

Wiki versus site glossaries

The definitions in a glossary need to be unassailable and absolutely reliable. After all, you are defining words, concepts, and skills that are in the course content, and they relate to the learning objectives. A wiki results in definitions of words and terms but, because it is collectively built, it may not be reliable. Even if it is reliable, some key terms may be missing and the definitions may be less than complete.

Main versus secondary glossaries

Each course can have only one main glossary, but it can have many secondary glossaries. The content of each secondary glossary shows up in the main glossary. This enables easy and clear-cut segregation of the contents in the main glossary.

The secondary glossary allows you to add a description of the glossary, and you can also customize it so that it says exactly what you'd like it to say:

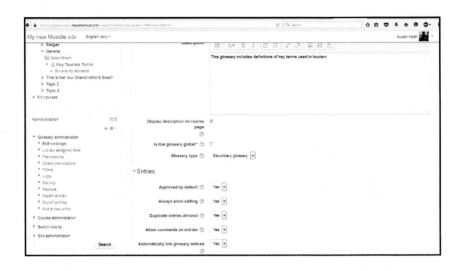

Managing students' contributions to a glossary

You can allow students to contribute to a glossary. Several features help you to manage this process.

By default, students can add new entries to a glossary. If you want to turn this off, you won't find it with the rest of the settings on the **Editing Glossary** page. Instead, you'll need to go to the **Roles** tab of the **Editing Glossary** page, select the **Override roles** sub tab, select the **Student** role, and take away this permission.

By default, **Duplicate entries allowed** is set to **No**. If you are allowing student contributions to a glossary, you might want to set this to **Yes**. If you forbid duplicates, you might want to assign your students to specific entries so that they do not try to create duplicates. You might also want to set **Allow comments on entries** to **Yes**, so that if a student can't create the entry they wanted to, the student can still comment on it.

Approved by default determines whether an entry created by a student is added to the glossary without the teacher's approval. If you've assigned each student specific glossary entries, you might want to set this to **No**. Then, when a student creates the assigned glossary entries, they appear under the **Waiting approval** tab of the glossary. This gives you a convenient place to check whether the student has completed the assignment. If you set this to **Yes**, then entries created by students go right into the glossary, and you need to search the entire glossary to determine whether a student has completed the assigned entries.

Edit always allows you to decide whether students can edit their entries at any time. If you set this to **Yes**, a student can always return to the entries they created and edit them. If you set this to **No**, a student cannot edit their entries after the editing time has passed. The editing time for a glossary is the same as for a forum posting. By default, Moodle gives a contributor 30 minutes to edit a glossary entry or forum posting before it is added. You can set this under site administration.

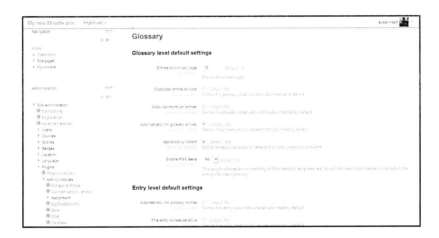

Ratings and comments

You can give students the ability to rate glossary entries, just like they can rate forum postings. The question is, which among the following do you want the students to rate:

- The clarity of the glossary entry
- Its helpfulness
- Your writing skill in creating the entry

You'll need to consider what you want students to rate, and create a custom scale that supports the rating. You determine who can rate glossary entries, and what scale to use, on the **Editing Glossary** page.

You must have read about creating a custom scale in the *Using a custom scale to rate relevance* subsection in `Chapter 2`, *Instructional Material*. Creating and applying a custom scale to glossary entries is the same as creating and applying it to forum entries.

Adding memory aids to glossary entries

Some subjects require memorization. This is a reality of teaching and learning. Vocabulary, formulae, and classifications all require students to memorize them. Reminders and mnemonics are memory aids that can make memorizing faster and easier for your students. Also, by creating clear categories and schemata, students will be able to organize the material.

Please remember that the mind recalls information when it goes from short-term memory to working memory. The memory retrieval process is facilitated by asking students to discuss the terms and concepts, and then to relate them to their own lives, experience, or prior knowledge.

One way to include memory aids in your course is to add them to glossary entries, as shown in the following screenshot:

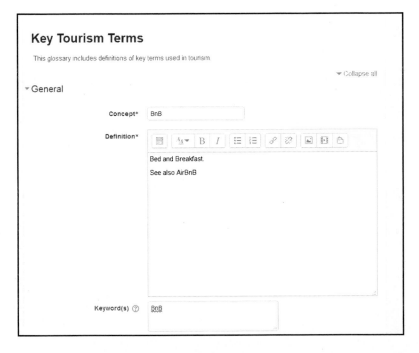

To add graphics, it is possible to click on the menu and directly insert a graphic file, link, video snippet, or other kind of graphic (maps and so on).

Student-created class directory

You can use a glossary for your class directory. Instruct the students to create a glossary entry for themselves. There are several things you can do to make this exercise easier for the students:

- First, create a page that the students can use as a template with placeholders for the information you want them to include. Also on this page, state the limitations for how personal the information can be.
- Consider leaving the **Edit always** function set to **Yes**. If a student wants to update their entry, or has second thoughts about some information they have included, the student should be able to easily edit the entry.
- If you ask students to include a picture in their glossary entry, give them directions for uploading and including pictures on a page. Although including a picture on a web page in Moodle is quite simple and similar to the way it's done on most blogging sites, include the directions anyway.
- You probably would want to turn off auto-linking for this glossary. If a student has the same name as another person who is studying in the course, or adds keywords that show up in the course, you would want a link to that student's glossary-biography to appear in the course.

If you assign this early in the course, students will gain practice with Moodle's online editor. The editor is the same for a glossary entry, page, or text assignment, so this practice can be very useful.

Student-created test questions

You can use a glossary to collect test questions from your students. Have them create test questions based on the work that they've done in class, and submit each question as a glossary entry.

Set **Approved by default** to **No**, unless you want students to see the questions that their classmates submit. Also, turn off automatic linking for the test question glossary.

After your students have submitted enough questions, you can pick the best entries for an exam.

Student-created extended definitions

You can use a glossary as a collaborative activity. In this case, it is similar to a wiki, but you can impose stricter guidelines and add very specific instructions.

For example, in the case of a definition of EcoTourism, students can contribute their own experiences and also add links to blog posts that illustrate their experiences. The student .can first add the official definition and then an example in a very succinct manner. Continuing with EcoTourism:

EcoTourism- Ecologically sustainable approach to tourism that targets places that are unique because of their ecology. The touristic experience focuses on active participation and has a goal of building cultural understanding, appreciation, and conservation.

Here is an example of protecting endangered sea turtle hatchlings in the Pacific coast town, Lo de Marcos, in Nayarit, Mexico. Here is a blog post I wrote about the experience (`http:/ /fringejournal.blogspot.in/2015/12/tortuga-twilight.html`):

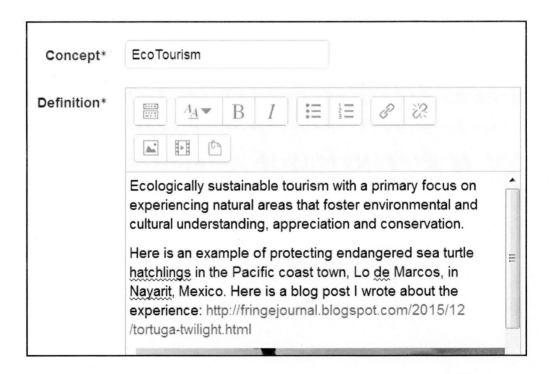

You can encourage students to add media, which could include images, audio, and video. This will further help illustrate their experience:

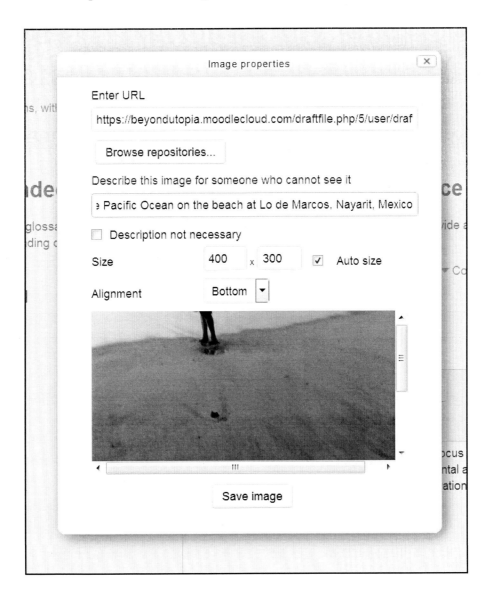

Summary

In this chapter, we discussed how Moodle's glossary function can be useful in developing learning activities that help achieve course outcomes, particularly those that require students to identify terms, discuss them, and apply their own experiences and ideas to solve problems or provide an analysis.

This chapter encouraged you to think beyond using the glossary just for vocabulary and, to use it to help students master key concepts. Keep in mind that many different pieces of information can be made into a glossary. It can be a collection of brief material such as descriptions, concepts, definitions, illustrative examples, quotes, tips, short stories, rules, policies, examples, frequently asked questions, diagrams, and even brief *"how to"* instructions. If you're going to create a web page with a list of items, ask yourself whether you could use a glossary instead.

The big advantage a glossary holds over a simple web page is its constant presence in the sidebar. With **Random Glossary Block**, you can put new information in front of the student every time they log into your course. The student doesn't need to click into a web page to see that information. Also, you can allow students to contribute to the glossary, which makes it an interactive activity. They can add personal experiences, links to blog posts, and also multimedia content, including images, audio, and video. Finally, be sure to build activities around the glossary and require students to discuss them in terms of the learning objectives that touch on the content.

8
The Choice Activity

Moodle's core philosophy involves the idea of active student engagement and participation. Forums allow students and instructors to interact with each other. Moodle's other activities foster other types of interactivity, and they enable students to vote on items, share opinions, and respond to polls. Instructors can capture the learners' interest to gauge progress, obtain feedback from learners, and facilitate communication within the group. Perhaps, the most important thing about Moodle is that it has an activity that helps you engage your readers, capture their interest, and then help them make sure that they are on track to achieve the desired course outcomes and individual learning objectives.

Polls, surveys, questionnaires, opinions, and *comprehension checks* can motivate students and make them feel involved and a part of a supportive and encouraging learning community. Plus, you can pique their curiosity with a *Check Your Understanding* or a *Did You Know?* question. You can be quirky, humorous, and even a little unexpected as you challenge the knowledge (and often the underlying assumptions) of your learners. While you may not initially think that polls and other interactive surveys could be a part of an online class as you start to implement them, you may find that they are one of the most popular elements within your course. Not only are people intrigued by unusual facts, they're also curious to see how their opinion stacks up in relation to their peers.

In this chapter, we will review Moodle's activities. The choice activity, specifically, can help you gauge your students' attitudes and activities, encourage participation, measure satisfaction and confidence, and trigger a desire to learn.

Moodle's choice activity

Moodle's choice is the simplest type of activity. In this activity, you create one question and specify a choice of responses:

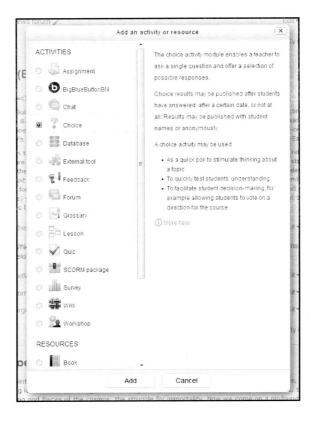

You can use a choice to:

- Take a quick poll
- Check their understanding of a topic or theme
- Pique their curiosity about a topic or skill covered in the course
- Ask students to choose sides in a debate
- Confirm the students' understanding of an agreement

The choice activity is also good for choosing meeting or appointment times between students and the professor or mentor. To do this, it is effective to limit the number of responses and then set the limit on each choice to 1. Each choice is a date and time of an available appointment. Each person can then choose an appointment time. It can be an effective way for staff who usually have to organize signup sheets to schedule appointments with their students:

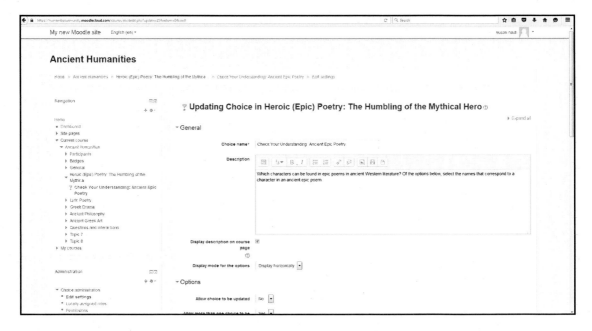

Before we look at how to accomplish this, let's look at the choice activity from the student's point of view, and then explore the settings available to the teacher while creating a choice.

A look at the choice activity

Before we discuss some of the uses of a choice activity, let's look at a *choice* from both the students' and teachers' point of view.

Students' point of view

From the students' point of view, a choice activity looks like this:

Check Your Understanding: Ancient Epic Poetry

View 0 responses

Which characters can be found in epic poems in ancient Western literature? Of the options below, select the names that correspond to a character in an ancient epic poem.

☐ Gilgamesh ☐ Aeneas ☐ Pinocchio ☐ Achilles ☐ Agamemnon

Save my choice

Note that at the bottom of the window, the student can see how many other students have chosen a response. There is also a limit on the number of students who can choose each response.

Teachers' point of view

Before we discuss some of the uses of a choice activity, let's consider the settings available on the **Editing Choice** page. We will then see how we can make creative use of these capabilities. Note that you can choose whether to allow one or more choices, and this affects the shape of the radio buttons, which are either round or square.

Number of choices

When you first use the **Editing Choice** page, Moodle gives you space for seven responses, and you can add up to three more:

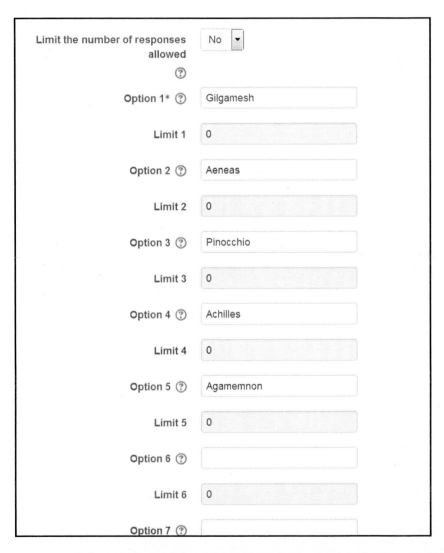

If you have used up all the choices and need more, you need to click on the **Add 3 fields to form** button.

Limit

The Limit option next to each choice enables you to limit how many students can select that choice. As shown in the preceding screenshot, not more than four students can select each choice. So after four students have selected **Choice 1**, that choice becomes unavailable. Limits must be enabled for the choice by clicking on **Enable** as shown in the following screenshot:

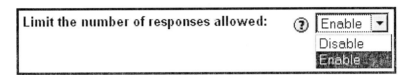

Publishing results

You can choose whether to reveal the results of the choice to the students by choosing an option from the drop-down menu, as shown in the following screenshot:

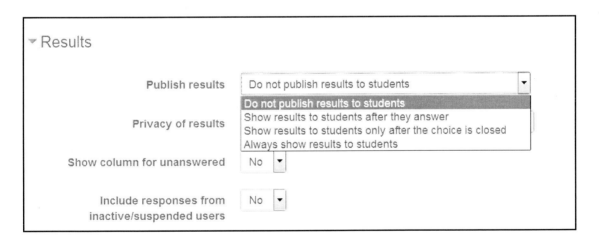

In the example at the beginning of this section, **Publish results** was set to **Always show results to students**. That is why the student could see how many students had chosen each response. If it had been set to **Do not publish results to students**, the activity would not have shown the number of students who selected each response.

Our public speaking class will end with a debate between three sides. The topic for the debate is the the legalization of illegal immigrants. The three sides are listed below.
Pick a side in the debate. There are twelve people in class. Each side is limited to four people.
You don't need to pick a side that you agree with. You can often learn more from supporting a view that you disagree with.

○ Illegal immigrants should be immediately located and deported.

○ We should implement a guest worker program where illegal immigrants can eventually earn their legal status.

○ We should declare amnesty for current illegal immigrants and allow them to apply for citizenship.

[Save my choice]

If you are going to limit the number of students who can choose a response, consider using **Always show results to students**. That way, the student can see how many people have chosen the response and how many slots are left for each response.

Privacy

If you publish the results of the choice, you can then choose whether to publish the names of the students who have selected each response:

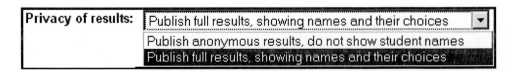

Privacy of results: | Publish full results, showing names and their choices ▼
Publish anonymous results, do not show student names
Publish full results, showing names and their choices

In the example at the beginning of this section, **Privacy of results** was set to **Publish anonymous results, do not show student names**. If it had been set to **Publish full results, showing names and their choices**, the student would have seen who had selected each response.

Allowing students to change their minds

The **Allow choice to be updated** setting determines if a student can change his/her answer after submitting it. If this is set to **Yes**, a student can retake the choice activity until the activity is closed.

Student polls

A great way to get students engaged and interested in their lessons is to ask their opinion and to make them participate in a poll. Giving students a chance to express their opinions may make them more curious about their assignments.

There are a number of excellent ways to enhance the learning experience and start forging a learning community.

- Build on the poll to create questions for a discussion forum
- Connect questions to practice quizzes
- Create a link to engage videos and audio that reinforce and support learning objectives

Learning styles

In addition to helping students feel connected and gauging the level of comprehension, engagement, and interest, the choice activity can be used to create questionnaires and psychological inventories. While you may not want to go into depth with something such as a Meyers-Briggs inventory, you may wish to help students identify certain characteristics or preferences, which could include learning styles.

So, you can use the choice activity to construct inventories that help students gain insight and understanding into their own processes. With new knowledge and insight, they may have more success in an online course as they adapt their study habits to accommodate their learning styles.

The Way I Prefer to Learn

View 0 responses

Here is a great place to match the way you like to learn with the kinds of activities that are available in the course. Please check the options that correspond to the way you learn best.

☐ Working in a team on a project   ☐ Watching a brief video

☐ Giving me a chance to tell a story and connect to my prior knowledge

☐ Listening to a lecture   ☐ Reading an article

Save my choice

After the students have indicated their learning preferences, you can code the course materials so that they correspond to the options in *The Way I Prefer to Learn*.

Self-regulation

Online student success often has a great deal to do with how a student is able to manage his/her own behaviors and to self-regulate. Self-regulation covers many aspects of one's life that pertain to education, particularly online learning. For example, self-regulation can include time management. A choice activity that involves a questionnaire to help students develop an understanding of their time management abilities can be very helpful as they modify their study approaches.

Choosing teams

You can use a choice activity to have students organize themselves into teams, as in the example that we've been using:

If you use a choice for this, there are some settings that will help your students. These are as follows:

- First, you might want to use the **Limit** setting to set a limit on the number of students who choose each team. This ensures that each team contains the same number of students.
- You will then probably want to set a **Time Limit** on the activity. Instruct the students that, if they don't choose a side within the given time, you will assign them one.
- Finally, you may want to publish the results to the students. If you select **Always show results to students**, the students will be able to see if any team is short on members. By turning on the **Allow choice to be updated** setting, you can give the students the ability to spontaneously organize themselves into teams of approximately equal size.

Under **Privacy of results**, you can choose to show the students' names and results, if you don't mind them choosing teams based on friendship and compatibility. If learning to work with people who they might not like is one of your learning goals, you might want to publish the results anonymously instead.

Students' consent

You can use a choice activity to confirm the students' understanding of an agreement or to record their consent. For example, if you're teaching a film-making class and you anticipate entering the resulting film into student competitions, you can use a choice to record the students' consent to have their work submitted to the competition or you can write the course syllabus and schedule as the text of the choice, and have the student confirm that he/she has read the syllabus. In this case, you might want the choice to have only one response, indicating the student's agreement. If you have a response indicating the student's disagreement, enable them to change their response and decide how you will handle the disagreement.

You can also use a choice to survey the class about their readiness to proceed with an activity. This is especially useful if the class needs to coordinate their efforts. For example, if you're using one of Moodle's workshop activities, you can have students assess each other's work as part of their grade. If some students don't submit their work on time, this can hold up the entire activity. To ensure students understand the workshop and are ready to start, you can use a survey to quickly poll them. When the entire class has responded that they are ready, you can proceed with the activity.

Students' performance

Consider creating a variety of choices to ask students about the pace, direction, and progress of your course. You can hide or reveal them whenever you want to poll the students. Place this kind of poll at the top of the page, under a heading to draw attention to it.

Preview the final

As a choice activity is not an official *quiz*, it can provide a non-threatening way to check the students' understanding of key concepts. Try preparing a variety of choice activities with questions about the most difficult concepts in a lesson, and using them to take quick measurements of how well the students are assimilating the material. Or create a series of choices called *Final Exam Questions*; tell students that each of these questions will appear in the final exam, in a slightly different form, and that each will have a time limit. When the student reads the newest question, he/she is rewarded with the answer to the previous question. This can motivate students to frequently check their progress in the course.

Summary

Moodle's Choice module is not only simple, but also very flexible. Its interface is less threatening than a quiz, and its publishing features allow students to see the progress of a choice, unlike a survey. Further, it is flexible and it allows you to engage students and encourage them to participate, making them feel that their opinions are being valued and that they are a part of the learning community. The choice activity can also be used for questionnaires and surveys that help identify learning preferences and styles, as well as time management and other areas of self-regulation that are critical to online success. Whenever you need to gather a feedback, gain a consensus, or take a poll, consider using a choice activity, which can also be accessed via the mobile app.

9

Course Solutions

An object-oriented design approach allows you to create components and to mix and match, reuse, and deploy them in multiple applications. Because it is easy to create components and to save them for reuse, it is sometimes easy to lose sight of the big picture. In this chapter, we'll discuss how to put it all together and create a very easy-to-teach and easy-to-navigate course.

Building the course design document

As you start to configure your course, please think of this course as a template and a guide for the courses you'll use in the future. By developing a template, you can start to build a course design document. You will be surprised by how easily you can develop a unique framework that has a particular look and feel, that is, your own brand.

Start by adding a course from the **Course Administration** menu and configuring it so that it can be modified for the future courses in your program, certificate, or degree:

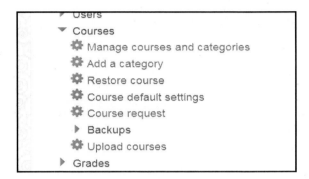

As you start to develop the courses, plan well so that the sequences, course names, course numbers, and descriptions are consistent and fit within a series of courses.

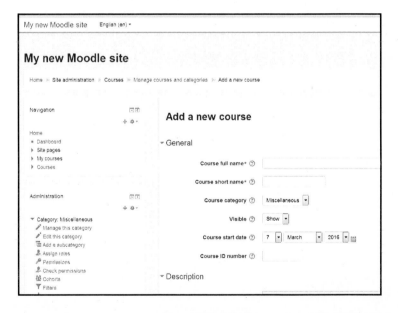

A good way to start is to think of the configuration of your course and the *flow*. How do you want your students to move through the course? How do you want your students to interact with you and their fellow students? The best way to start is to begin with the homepage.

By default, every course has a **Topic 0** at the top of the course's homepage. This topic is intended to hold information about the course. We usually begin adding the content of the course with **Topic 1**. For example, if a course uses a *Weekly* format, every topic will be assigned to one week, but **Topic 0** will not have a date. If your course uses the *Topics* format, **Topic 1** and onwards will be numbered, but **Topic 0** will not be numbered. This indicates to the student that **Topic 0** is not part of the course flow.

There are several kinds of information that fit well into **Topic 0** of your course. In general, this is information that you want the student to see as soon as they enter the course. Remember that the student won't see **Topic 0** until after being enrolled, so don't include any information that the student might need before enrolling, such as the course description and prerequisites.

Prioritizing and selecting based on learning objectives

As you select activities to include in your course, be sure to keep in mind that you're facilitating the learning process and that your main goal is to help students achieve learning objectives.

Thus, be sure to arrange the course in a building block fashion and to use scaffolding so that the content blocks build on each other and that the sequence is logical.

Understanding your students, their technologies and their access

As you design your course, be sure to keep in mind the "real-world" realities of your students. What are their goals and interests? If you know that they are interested in ancient Greece, then you'll need to be sure to give them chances to have access to materials that help them achieve learning goals.

Also, keep in mind the kinds of access your students are likely to have. If they are not in the same time zone, be sure to build in asynchronous elements for the synchronous activities. For example, be sure to save and archive relevant Chat transcripts. If you use BigBlueButtonBN for web conferences or webinars, be sure to share and/or archive them so that students who are not able to participate *live* can go back and view them.

Tailoring your courses to meet the needs, interests, and technical realities of your students will help them feel comfortable and confident.

Overcoming course anxiety

If you've ever taught a class in person, you might have noticed that when students arrive for the first session they often look at the board and around the room for an indication that they have found the right room. Sometimes they even ask, *Is this the _____ class?* Online, students may have a similar experience.

Placing the course name at the very top of **Topic 0** can give them the same reassurance as writing the course name on the board at the front of the room:

Ancient Humanities

Home ▶ Ancient Humanities

Important announcements

By default, every course you create in Moodle is given a **Topic 0** with a **News forum** added.

The **Latest News** block is also automatically added. This block displays the latest announcement(s) added to the **News Forum**. You may also customize the title for the **News forum** or **Latest News** blocks. In the next screenshot, you can see the results:

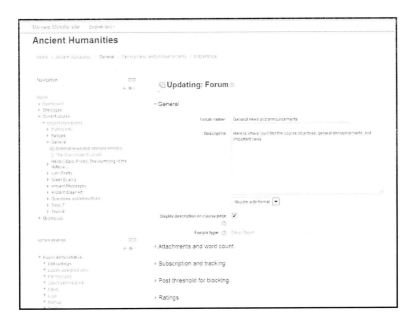

However, if the announcement is especially important, you might not want to count on your students to read the **Latest News** block. In these cases, consider using **Topic 0** for critical announcements. Note the announcement in the next screenshot and compare it with the previous screenshot:

In this example, the teacher added a label to **Topic 0**. The headline was formatted with the style Heading 3 so that it stands out from the general news and announcements tab. Then the label was positioned at the top of the topic.

Moving blocks to the main course area

The standard Moodle installation gives you the choice of two, one, or no side columns for your blocks. If you want to eliminate the side columns, you have more space for your course content, but no space for blocks. Let's explore a workaround for that. We'll use the **Participants** block as an example.

Normally, the **Participants** block would occupy one of the side columns, which is valuable screen space and can be used for the main course content. Now, what if we want to have the functionality of the block, without needing a side column? This is examined in the next section.

The goal

We want to arrive at a solution that looks like this:

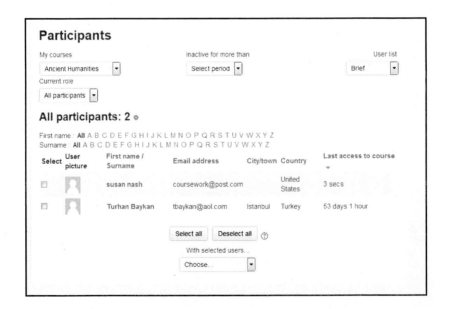

Note that, instead of having a **People** block in one of the side columns, the course displays a link to the **Participants** in the main course area.

You can see in the following screenshot the **Participants** link in the current course area and see that it takes you to **Course blogs**, **Notes**, and the User's personal page, where the User details, **Badges**, **Course details**, and **Roles** are found:

Home
- Dashboard
▶ Site pages
▼ Current course
  ▼ Ancient Humanities
    ▼ Participants
      - Course blogs
      - Notes
      - susan nash

Course blogs

Moodle 3.0 has incorporated a number of social media elements that are built in so that it's not necessary to embed code or create links to outside social media, such as blogs.

In the past, many Moodle administrators opted to use social media by building links within Moodle to Facebook, Twitter, Blogger, WordPress, and other sites.

Blogs were useful, but they created a security issue. Now, in Moodle 3.0, it's possible for students to blog about the course. It's possible for students to post a blog entry and then for other students to comment:

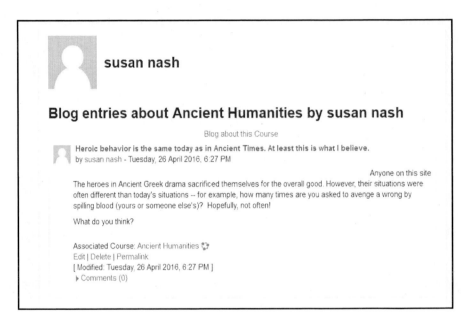

Notes

Moodle 3.0 also allows you to create notes on the course and to use them. It's very convenient because your notes stay with the course and you don't have to worry about where you might have stored them, either on a flash drive or in the cloud in a service such as Dropbox or Evernote.

When you click on **Notes**, you'll be taken to the user page.

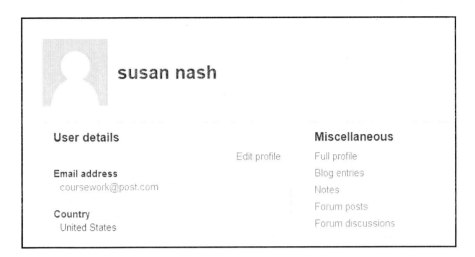

Then, you can click on **Notes** and start typing the notes. Your thoughts will be saved with the day of the week, date, and time, which can help you keep track of your thoughts and the development of your ideas.

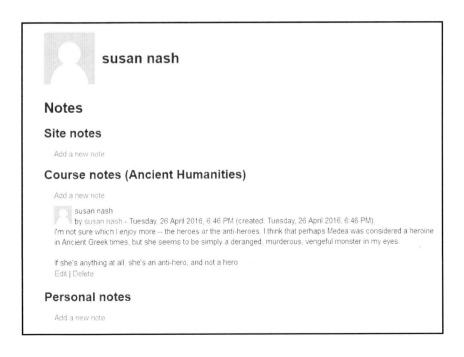

General news and announcements – learning objectives

The General news forum is an excellent place to post your learning objectives. You can post them and then encourage students to post questions or responses to them.

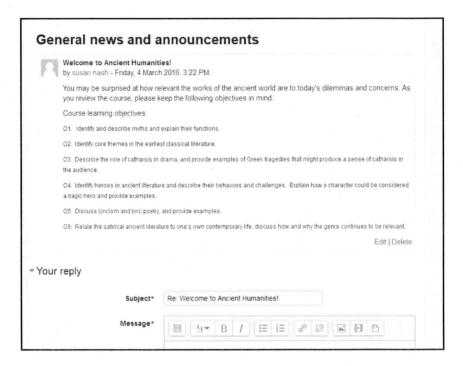

It is also a good place to post general announcements, such as changes in deadlines or notices about the course.

Using this workaround with other blocks

You can copy any link generated by a block and paste it into the main area of your course. Then, you can hide the block and eliminate the side column that would have held that block. However, you will need to experiment with each link to determine whether it works.

Section Links

The **Section Links** block creates a link to each visible section in your course.

Note that the links are just numbers; they do not give you the title of each section. You can copy each of these links and place them in **Topic 0** and then label each link. It would look like this:

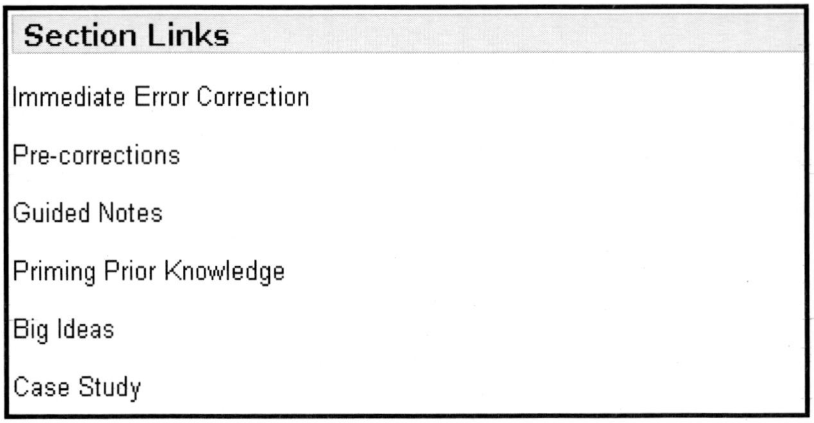

Section Links

Immediate Error Correction

Pre-corrections

Guided Notes

Priming Prior Knowledge

Big Ideas

Case Study

When using this method to create section links, you must remember two things:

- First, as mentioned earlier, these links are static. They will not be updated if you move your course. If you are working on a development server, make these links for your production server.
- Second, while creating the link in Moodle for the **Target**, select **Same frame**.

This makes the link open in the same window and frame. The effect is that the page scrolls down to the section.

Activities

The **Activity modules** block displays links to each kind of activity in your course, as shown in the following screenshot:

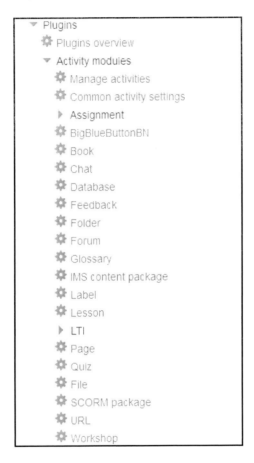

Clicking on any of these links displays all of the activities of that type in your course. For example, clicking on the **Assignments** link displays the following:

Week	Name	Assignment type	Due date	Submitted	Grade
1	Example: Immediate Error Correction in an Assignment	Upload a single file	Tuesday, 6 February 2007, 05:00 PM	View 1 submitted assignments	-
	Practice: Create a Lesson with Remedial Information	Offline activity	Thursday, 8 February 2007, 05:00 PM	View 0 submitted assignments	-
2	Practice Part 1: Create a Workshop with Teacher Example	Offline activity	Tuesday, 13 February 2007, 05:00 PM	View 0 submitted assignments	-
	Pactice Part 2: Assess Another Student's Teacher Example	Offline activity	Thursday, 15 February 2007, 05:00 PM	View 0 submitted assignments	-
	Practice Part 3: Assess Your Student's Work	Offline activity	Friday, 16 February 2007, 05:00 PM	View 0 submitted assignments	-

If an activity type appears in your course, a link to that type appears in the block. If your course does not have a given type of activity, then a link to that type will not be displayed. For example, if your course does not have any assignments, then the **Assignments** link will not appear in the block. If you add an activity type to a course, then the block is dynamically updated with that type of activity.

You can copy the links from this block and place them in your main course area. Then you can hide the block and possibly eliminate the sidebar that it occupied. However, as noted before, the block is dynamically updated if you add a new type of activity to your course.

The syllabus

Including a link to the course syllabus from **Topic 0** is almost obvious. We suggest two refinements to your syllabus.

Printer-friendly for letter and A4 sizes

First, make the syllabus printer-friendly. Even though we live in *the computer age,* many people still prefer to have a hardcopy of their schedules and tasks. Providing the syllabus in PDF format makes it easier for students to generate a printout.

If you have students in both North America and the rest of the world, you will want the printout to be formatted so that it prints well on both Letter and A4-sized paper. Letter-sized paper is shorter than A4, at 11 inches (279.4 mm). A4-sized paper is narrower than Letter, at 8.27 inches (210 mm). Ensure that content doesn't go outside the printable area of the paper, by using margins of 0.5 inches to keep the material inside that area. This will take care of the top, left, and right margins for students who are using both A4 and Letter paper.

As A4 is 0.7 inches (18 mm) longer than Letter, use hard page breaks to give an additional 0.7 inches of space between the last line of your page and the margin. That will make the document print properly on Letter-size paper. So the space between the last text on a page and the bottom of the page will be 1.2 inches, with a 0.5 inch margin and another 0.7 inch due to the hard page break.

Online calendar with event reminders

Google, Yahoo!, 30 Boxes (`http://30boxes.com/welcome.php`), and others offer online calendars that you can open to the public. These online calendars can be accessed with desktop calendars such as Outlook, iCal, Evolution, KOrganizer, and Sunbird. For example, students can access my course calendar on Google by subscribing via an XMLS feed, iCal subscription, or by viewing an HTML page:

Most online calendars can send reminders of events via e-mail. Sending a reminder of an assignment the day before it's due can be a good way to help your students stay on schedule. However, most online calendars can send reminders to only one e-mail address. To send reminders to all of the students in the class, consider using an online group such as Google+ or Facebook. However, your administrator may not allow social media, so be sure to check whether social media sharing is permitted.

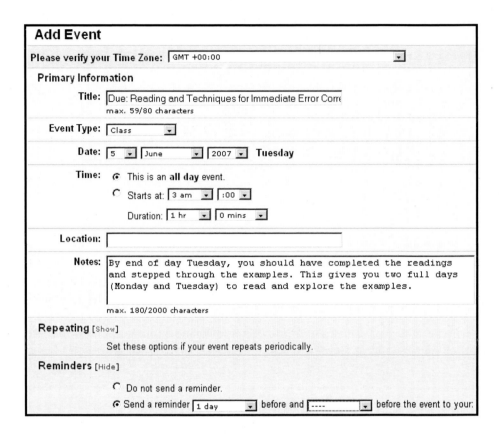

Note that the event is actually an assignment, which is due on that day. Refer to **Due: Reading and Techniques for Immediate Error Correction** in the previous screenshot. Also notice that under the **Reminders** section, I'm sending an e-mail reminder to everyone in the group one day before. Students, who choose to join this group will receive an e-mail reminder for each assignment when it is due.

Encouraging course completion

People often fail to complete because they are not motivated. We can build in course completion strategies through using Choice (engages), Quizzes, Certificates, and Badges.

For example, as you create the course template, you can build in an engager using the Choice activity.

In addition, you can tie the learning objectives to quizzes and giving one to check knowledge.

Certificates and Badges are great ways for students to show their knowledge for their work, future employer, and professional association.

Webinars and web conferences can be conducted via BigBlueButton.

Creating certificates

Certificates can be generated at the end of the course and can reflect participation and/or a passing or mastery grade. In the case of mastery learning, the certificate is generated upon completing quizzes with more than 80 percent. Students generally have unlimited attempts.

The Certificate module creates customizable certificates in PDF format for students in a course. You can customize them by adding borders, watermarks, seals, signatures, outcomes, grades, and custom text to a certificate.

You can download the Certificate module from the download plugins at `https://moodle.org/plugins/`. If your administrator has already downloaded the Certificate modules, you'll find them in your **Site Administration Plugin** menu:

The certificate downloads should match the Moodle version that you are using. You can also use Badges, which they can then display in their social media.

Creating Badges

Badges are similar to certificates in the sense that they reward performance in a course. They can be presented to employers and others who are important to the students.

Badges go a step further because they are intended to be displayed via social media and thus the accomplishments of the student can be made public via Facebook, LinkedIn, blogs, or other places where they like to display their profile and accomplishments.

Badges are listed in the **Site Administration** menu under **Advanced Features**. You can standardize the settings for all the **Badges** generated. You can also manage **Badges** (after you've added **Badges**) and add a new **Badge**.

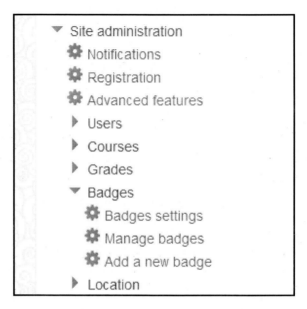

As you configure the **Badge**, you can customize the images and also the name:

After you have selected the name, the image, and details for the **Badge**, you can upload an image. Then, once you've configured the **Badge**, you can set the criteria by which it is issued. Here is an example for **Ancient Humanities**. Notice that I've included a photo of the Parthenon that I obtained from Wikimedia Commons. I can also create my own graphic and upload it.

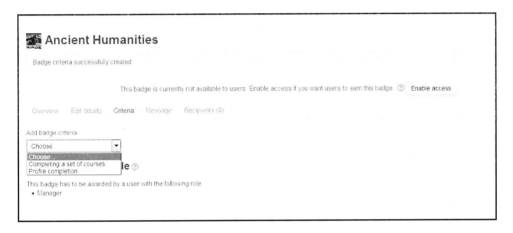

After you've created the **Badge**, be sure to make it available for users. Once individuals start earning **Badges**, encourage them to display them. It will be a point of pride!

They can also display them in the Open Badges project, located here: `https://backpack.openbadges.org/backpack/login`.

Motivating interaction via webinars and web conferencing

Web conferences and webinars have become very popular ways of transferring knowledge. In addition to providing synchronous, or *live* interaction, webinars and web conferences can be archived and then accessed on demand for students who may wish to watch the recording again and also leave comments in a discussion forum.

Moodle uses BigBlueButtonBN for web conferencing. It is a plugin and can be installed from the plugins menu in **Site Administration**. After you select the **BigBlueButtonBN** option, you have an opportunity to configure it. By default, it is necessary to wait for the moderator in order to start recording. This is an important point because, if you do not wait for the moderator, you may have a bit of chaos.

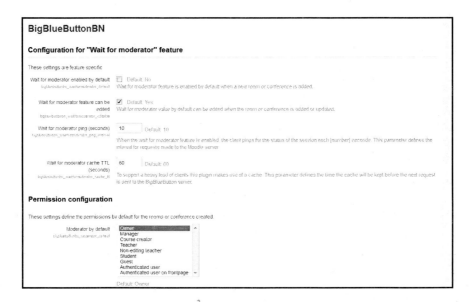

I've configured **BigBlueButtonBN** so that it appears on the homepage for the course, **Ancient Humanities**. It appears under the News forum area, so that it's easy for the students to see.

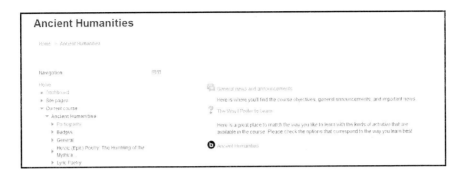

Once the moderator launches BigBlueButtonBN, you'll be directed to an external site where the web conference will take place. You can use internal microphones for audio and can also turn on the web camera so that the moderator, and also other participants, can use their web cameras to customize the experience.

One cautionary note, however. If you're going to enable the web camera for all the participants, you'll need very good connection speed and bandwidth. I'm excited about BigBlueButtonBN and Moodle. It's easy to use, very reliable, and a wonderful addition to Moodle, which makes it unnecessary to rely on external vendors for a web conferencing solution.

Summary

In this chapter, the solutions focused on developing a template you can use again, which is also your design document. As you start to build the structure of the course, you will focus on making your course easier to navigate. The goal of all these solutions is to reduce the time and effort your students spend figuring out what to do next, so that they can get on with learning. **Topic 0** is useful for introductory information and for keeping students up-to-date with current announcements. Moving blocks to the main course area eliminates the sidebars and frees space for course content. An online syllabus with e-mail reminders helps keep your students on schedule. Incorporating activities that motivate students is important and they can range from awarding certificates and badges, to involving students in interactive web conferences and webinars.

Sometimes, reducing the effort the students need to make in order to navigate through your course requires a great deal of effort on your part. Anything you do to help your students navigate easily through your course is worth the effort. The result is less time spent wondering what to do next and more time spent on your course content.

10
Workshop Solution

People learn from each other. When people react to each other's ideas, they start to relate knowledge to the course concepts, prior knowledge, and the world at large. They are often surprised to find that they remember the items and elements they have discussed with each other long after the course is over.

As we have seen in previous chapters, one of Moodle's strengths is that it is very flexible and it encourages you to develop courses that are highly interactive. Moodle's object-oriented approach lets you develop individual components, which you can put into different applications. At the same time, the tools and activities within Moodle encourage peer interaction.

One of the most effective approaches is to put together a Moodle Workshop. It is an activity that focuses on interaction, collaboration, and application of the knowledge learned. The workshop allows:

- Application of knowledge by creating a project
- Collaboration with peers to amend or revise the project
- Interaction with peers to share ideas and concepts
- Revision and expansion of projects

As you will see, the workshop has numerous components that can help you guide students and help them develop and share their ideas, make revisions, and constantly interact, test, probe, and explore what they are learning. In doing so, they will learn critical thinking skills as well as persuasive arguments and presentation skills.

This chapter will take you through the process of creating a fully featured workshop. It will not cover workshop administration, as Moodle's online documentation does an adequate job of explaining that. Instead, this chapter will focus on helping you make decisions that create the kind of workshop experience you want your students to undergo.

Workshop overview and use

Moodle's Workshop module is one of the most complex and powerful of all the activities. A workshop provides a place where students can:

1. Receive directions for completing a project.
2. View an example of a completed project provided by the teacher.
3. Assess the teacher's example using criteria given by the teacher.
4. Compare their assessment of the example to the teacher's assessment of the same example.
5. Submit their completed project.
6. Assess other students' completed projects, again using the criteria given by the teacher.
7. Compare their assessment of other students' work to the assessments made by other students and by the teacher.
8. Receive assessments of the project that they have submitted.

We listed the workshop tasks in the order students usually complete them. You can skip some of these steps. However, the steps that can be skipped offer the most educational benefit.

For example, you can skip Steps 3 and 4. If you do that, the workshop becomes a matter of just reading instructions on how to complete a project, viewing an example, and submitting the work. You might as well just use an Assignment instead. Assessing an example gives the student a clear idea about the teacher's expectations. Comparing their assessment to an assessment made by the teacher confirms or denies the student's understanding of the expectations. This step is especially important if the student will be assessing other students' work.

Step 6 is also optional, but this can result in missed opportunities for learning. When a student is asked to assess another student's work, instead of just reading or reviewing it, the assessor is probably paying more attention to detail and spending more time on the work.

Steps 7 and 8 are also optional. As a teacher, you could just assess each student's work yourself. However, allowing a student to be assessed by others, and having them see how others assessed the work that they assessed, makes the workshop a powerful collaborative experience.

Workshops and collaborative solutions

Moodle allows you to easily incorporate activities that require students to collaborate. The Workshop solution is just one of them, and it is particularly useful because it is flexible and easily customizable.

The Workshop allows students to collaborate and also to assess each other's work. Work can be submitted in stages, and the students have the opportunity to contribute and also to evaluate/assess each other.

The value of collaboration is that it can encompass many different ways of learning and can accommodate many different learning styles. You can trigger emotional connections, incorporate prior learning, and connect to other subject areas. Further, you can incorporate strategies that accommodate visual, auditory, kinesthetic, and other preferred learning styles.

Workshop basics

Workshops are complex. There are many components and most settings that you choose will affect or be affected by at least one or the other setting. Let's review some basic concepts before we talk about workshop specifics.

Listing your learning objectives

It is easy to get a bit carried away and to start building a Workshop before you have a clear purpose in mind. While this is fine if you're simply putting together a framework or a design document, it is not very effective if you're going to implement your Workshop and use it to train others.

As you develop the activities, focus them on learning objectives. It is often useful to refer to Bloom's taxonomy as you develop the cognitive tasks you will incorporate. Be sure to include different levels of complexity, from simple identification to higher-level tasks such as evaluation.

Planning your strategy

When you create a Moodle workshop, you may enter several pages worth of information. Again, think of learning objectives. At the same time, consider that all the settings that you choose can be summarized into some basic questions:

- What work do you want the student to submit?
- Will a student assess the work of their classmates; if so, how will that affect the student's grade?
- To what extent does a student's grade depend on assessing their peers' performance, and how much of the work the student has submitted?
- What are the criteria for assessing the work?
- What submissions will the student assess: an example by the teacher, other students' work, and/or the student's own submission?
- If classmates assess each other's work, will they do this anonymously?
- Is it necessary for classmates to agree on a grade or can they make their assessments independent of each other?
- What is the schedule for submitting the work and for submitting assessments?

Try to answer these questions before you begin creating your workshop. When you have answered them, you have created your workshop strategy. Then as we step through creating a workshop, we will equate each setting with one of the questions.

Grading peer assessment

One of the most unique features of a workshop is that the student doesn't receive a grade only for the work that they have submitted; the student can also receive a grade for the assessments that they have performed. In other words, a student is graded on the grades that they give to others. With peer assessment, students have additional opportunities for engagement.

Keep in mind that you can assign grades based on the number of responses, and ask students to be productive and supportive.

Getting started – setting up the Workshop

In Moodle 3.0 Workshops are very easy to set up. The **Workshop** is an activity module, and appears in the activity menu.

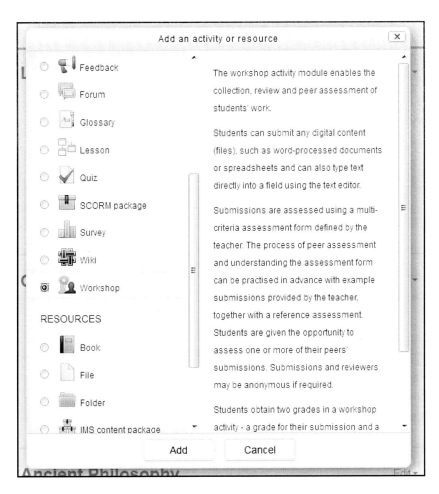

Let's set up a **Workshop** that allows our students to work individually and to collaborate in creating and assessing creative writing. In this case, the students will review the recently discovered manuscript fragments written by Sappho, the ancient Greek poetess, and they will attempt to reconstruct and recreate the work. They will *fill in the gaps* missing in the manuscript, where words do not appear.

Then, the students will read each other's invented manuscripts and will assess them.

Let's start by adding a new workshop to our **Ancient Humanities** course. It will fit in the, **Lyric Poetry** unit.

- In the **Workshop name** field, enter the name of the Workshop. Students will see this on the course homepage.
- **Description** field. This field can be a description of the Workshop and/or instructions for completing the work. The following example illustrates some of the key elements of a Workshop description
  - The goal of the Workshop. This is in the first sentence.
  - An overview of what the student will do. This is in the second and third paragraphs.
  - Step-by-step directions for completing the Workshop. This example could be improved if the author included a link to a printer-friendly version of the instructions.
  - A clear statement of what to do first. This is in the last sentence.

After we have added the Workshop, let's establish the **Grading settings**. In this case, we will use **Accumulative grading** because we want to encourage continuous and ongoing participation.

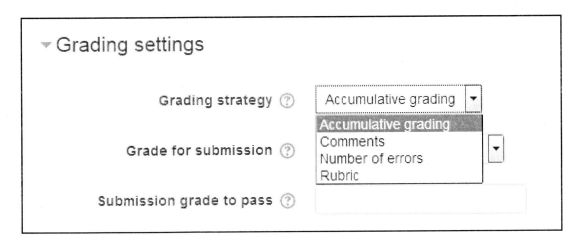

In order to make sure that the students know exactly what to do, we will provide customized instructions for submissions. You will write the instructions in the box.

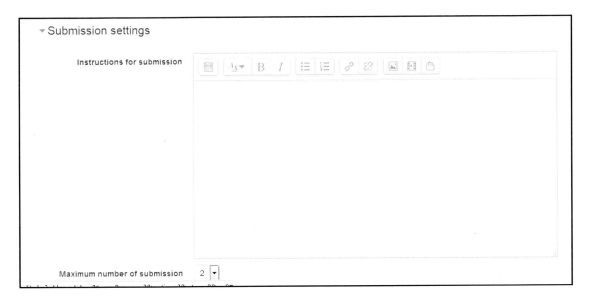

You can expand or modify your instructions by clicking on **edit** or the pencil icon. Here, I've added instructions. Notice that I've tried to give the sense of a game or puzzle to engage the learners and to pique their curiosity. In the workshop, it's important to maintain a sense of adventure or mystery.

The Workshop is a perfect place to deal with solving riddles and mysteries together. It is perfect for a forensics course.

In this workshop, we'll work together to review the scraps of manuscript attributed to the ancient Greek poet, Sappho. They are fragmentary and incomplete. It is your job to work with your team members to fill in the gaps and create full poems as Sappho would have written them.

The **Submission settings** screen gives you an opportunity to develop a clear set of instructions.

They will appear at the place where your students will submit their work, and thus are very clear.

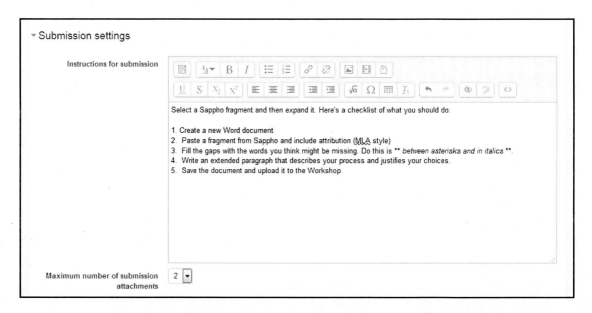

Select a Sappho fragment and then expand it. Here's a checklist of what you should do:

1. Create a new Word document
2. Paste a fragment from Sappho and include attribution (MLA style)
3. Fill the gaps with the words you think might be missing. Do this is ** between asterisks and in italics **.
4. Write an extended paragraph that describes your process and justifies your choices.
5. Save the document and upload it to the Workshop.

After you complete the instructions and you start to consider how they will work in real life, you can consider ways to incorporate students and shape their roles.

Moodle 3.0 makes it easy to define and assign roles. It can be useful for the teacher to also have a student role so that it is possible to switch between the two and make entries to get things started.

To make sure that you have completed all the required steps to set up a fully functioning Workshop, you can refer to a **Summary** screen that indicates where you are in the setup process.

Let's take a look at the Workshop **Expanding Sappho Fragments**. It is clear that the course is still in the setup phase and that there are a few items that can be modified before launching. For example, it's possible to edit the assessment form.

The **Summary** screen gives you a chance to review the **Assessment phase** and to see whether you've allowed enough time for assessment, and whether the dates are correct.

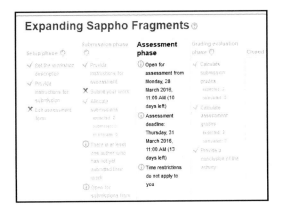

You can then set up the assessment form. Note that the "X" will change to a check mark when you complete the step. So, click on **Edit assessment form** to open the page and then include instructions.

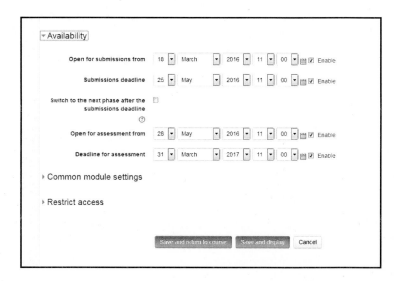

As you are editing the settings, you can configure the availability for submitting and assessing student work.

Step-by-step example – submissions

Understanding how to create submissions is a critical part of the process, and it is one where you are likely to receive questions. Let's start by going back to a workshop we've created and editing it.

Setting up a task

Here is an example of how you can set up a task. It could be an assignment for a class in photography. We'll start with the goal of the assignment. You can enter the goals and the instructions in the description box.

Here is an example of the text you can place in the description box:

In this assignment, you will explore the limitations of your lens' depth of field. You will take two pictures of a close-up subject. One picture will have a second subject in the medium background, six to eight feet from the lens. The other picture will have a second subject in the far background, over thirty feet from the lens. You will see the limitations in your lens's ability to simultaneously focus on a close-up subject and background subject. Before taking and submitting your pictures, you must review the two examples provided by the instructor. Click the **Assess link** below to display the assessment form, and the links to the examples. Your submissions will be graded by the teacher, using the same form.

Next, let's look at specific instructions. To complete this assignment, assess the two examples provided by the teacher. Take the first photo. Place the main subject no more than three feet from the lens and a second subject six to eight feet from the lens. Name this picture `yourname_close-med.jpg`, where `yourname` is your username.

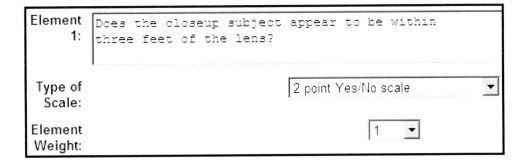

Take the second photo. Place the main subject no more than three feet from the lens, and a second subject thirty or more feet from the lens. Name this picture `yourname_close-far.jpg`, where `yourname` is your username.

Attach the two photos. Below you see a form titled **Submit your Assignment using this Form:** and after that you should see fields for **Attachment 1:** and **Attachment 2:.** Use those fields to attach your photos.

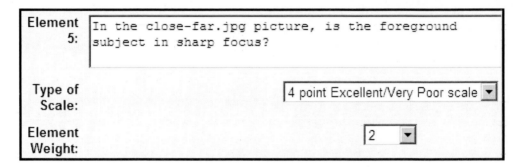

In the **Title:** field for the submission form, enter your username.

In the **Description:** field, for each picture, give the distance from the lens to the closest subject, the distance from the lens to the background subject, the lens opening used, and the focal length used.

Finally, submit the assignment.

In this example, I have given complete instructions for completing the Workshop. You might choose to enter a minimal description and put the instructions in a web page or a PDF file instead.

Assessing student peer assessment

For the **Grade for Assessments** field, select a value. This value is the maximum grade the student can earn for assessing the work of their peers, and for assessing their own work.

This is not a grade for the work the student submitted. This is a grade for the assessments the student completed. The teacher does not assign this grade. Instead, Moodle automatically calculates this grade.

The calculation happens in one of two ways. If the teacher assesses a submission, Moodle compares the student's assessment of that submission with the teacher's. The closer the student comes to matching the teacher's assessment, the higher the student's **Grade for Assessments**.

For example, if both Student 1 and the Teacher assessed the work of Student 2, and Student 1's assessment matched the Teacher's assessment almost exactly, then Student 1 would receive a high grade for that assessment.

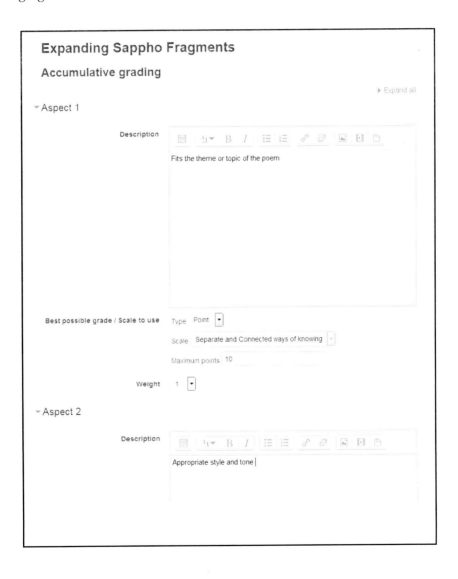

Or in case the teacher did not assess a submission, the student's assessment of that submission is compared with the assessments made by the other students in the class. The closer the assessment of the student is to the average, the better the student's grade is for that assessment. If a submission is assessed by one or two students, then that student receives the best grade possible for their assessment. If a submission is assessed by three or more students, then the student's grade is closer to the average.

If you want the student to be graded on how close their assessment is to those of their peers, then the teacher should not perform any assessments, and you should have the student assess three or more submissions. If you want the student to be graded on how close their assessment is to that of the teacher's, then of course the teacher will need to assess each submission.

Student grade – peer assessment and student work

Now you can determine how much of the student's grade depends on assessing the work of their peers, and how much work the student has submitted.

For the **Grade for Submission** field, select a value. This value is the maximum grade the student can earn for the work that they submit.

The grade for submission is determined by the assessments that the teacher and/or classmates made of the work. If the student's work is assessed by only the teacher, then the grade for submission is whatever the teacher determines. If the student's work is assessed by their classmates, then the grade for submission is determined by their assessments. If both the teacher and classmates assessed the work, then the grade is affected by both.

What are the criteria for assessing the work?

Select a grading strategy. It determines how the student's work will be assessed by their classmates. Earlier, on the **Editing Workshop** page, you selected the maximum **Grade for Submission**. When a student's submission is being assessed, the student gets a grade for the submission. All of the assessments for a submission will be averaged and the grade for the submission will be calculated. More on how the grade is calculated is discussed later.

The online help gives complete explanations for each grading strategy. In brief, your choices are:

- **Not Graded**: When a classmate assesses the student's work, they leave comments but do not grade them. Recall that previously we said the **Grade for Assessments** is calculated based on the scores a classmate gives when performing an assessment. If you select **Not Graded**, then a classmate does not give any scores when they perform an assessment. The result is that Moodle cannot calculate a **Grade for Assessments** when the **Grading Strategy** is set to **Not Graded**. This would seem to put us in a quandary. If we base a part of each student's grade on the assessments that they perform, but the assessments consist only of comments that Moodle cannot use to calculate a grade, how do we get a grade for the assessments? In this case, the teacher can grade the student's assessments. The maximum points that the teacher can give for this grade are set in the **Grade for Assessments**.

- **Accumulative grading**: In this strategy, the teacher creates several assessment elements. Each element is a specific, well-defined criterion for judging the work and each element can have its own grading scale. For example, here is an assessment element from a photography workshop. Note that in the following screenshot it uses a 2-point scale, and has an **Element Weight** of **1** point:

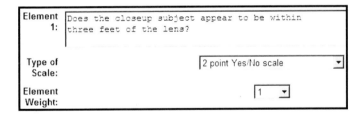

- Here is another assessment element from the same workshop. Note that this one uses a 4-point scale, and has an **Element Weight** of **2** points:

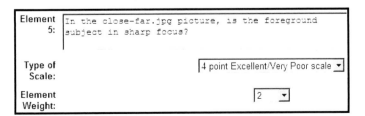

- **Number of errors grading**: The submission is assessed using a set of Yes/No criteria. Using **Number of errors** grading, an assessment element would look like this:

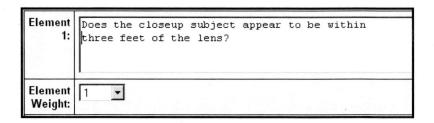

Note the default **Element Weight** is **1**.

What submissions will the student assess

A student can assess any number of items: an example by the teacher, other students' work, and/or the student's own submission.

If the **Number of Assessments of Examples from Teacher** setting is set to a number other than 0, the student must assess examples provided by the teacher before they can upload a submission.

Select a value for **Comparison of Assessments.** Remember that previously you chose a **Grade for Assessments**. Recall that, if the teacher assesses the submissions, then a student's grade for assessments is calculated by comparing it to the teacher's assessments. If the teacher does not assess the submissions, then a student's grade for assessments is calculated by comparing it to the assessments made by the rest of the class. This setting determines how closely the student's assessment must agree with the teacher's, or with the class average, for a submission. For example, if this is set to **Very Lax**, and there are 10 yes/no assessment criteria, an assessment that agrees with the teacher on 8 of the 10 criteria would earn a grade of 80%. But if it is set to **Very Strict**, it would earn a grade of 35%.

The **Number of Assessments of Student Submissions** setting determines how many submissions each student will be asked to assess. If this is set to 0, then students do not assess each other's work.

Recall that the grade is calculated from the assessments made of that submission. **Weight for Teacher Assessments** determines how much the teacher's assessment affects that grade. You select how many student assessments the teacher's assessment is worth. If this is set to 0, the teacher's assessment is not used when determining a student's grade for submissions.

As students submit or upload their work to a workshop, Moodle allocates it to other students for assessment. The field **Number of Assessments of Student Submissions** determines how many submissions each student is required to assess. Ideally, everyone will submit their assignments on time, and students will have plenty of time to evaluate each other's work. For example, suppose there are 10 students in the class, and **Number of Assessments of Student Submissions** is set to **3**. That means each of the 10 submissions is assessed three times. Moodle assigns the assessments as the work is submitted manually.

However, if a student submits work late, the students who are going to evaluate the late person's work will need to wait before they can complete their assessments. Let's suppose one student doesn't submit their work by the deadline. That means the class is three assessments short. As Moodle assigns the assessments evenly, three students will end the class one assessment short. Shall we penalize these students for not completing the required three assessments?

In our example, **Over Allocation** is set to 0, and each submission is evaluated three and only three times. If we set **Over Allocation** to 1, then, when the deadline arrives, Moodle will over allocate some work to the students who still need to complete their assessments. In this example, Moodle will randomly choose three pieces of work that have already been assessed three times, and assign them to the three students who are missing an assessment. These pieces of work will then be over allocated by one assessment each. Moodle allows a maximum **Over Allocation** of **2**.

If **Self Assessment** is set to **Yes**, each student is asked to evaluate their own work. This is in addition to the number of student submissions that the student is asked to evaluate.

Anonymous assessments

If **Assessments must be agreed** is set to **Yes**, then an assessment made by one student can be viewed by the other reviewers of the same work. If the other reviewers disagree, the evaluation process continues until they agree or until the assignment's closing time is passed. This can be a useful tool for determining how clear your evaluation elements are. If there is a lot of disagreement among reviewers of the same work, revisit your evaluation elements and the instructions you gave the reviewers.

In many cases, it is better to simply assign grades based on participation. Ask your students to give positive comments. Their ideas should always relate to the learning objectives, and the goal should be to help students be more self-confident. This is a good place to develop a rubric to guide student comments.

Classmate agreement on grades

You may customize the assessment, depending on whether or not students must agree on a grade or whether they must make their assessments independent of each other.

The **Hide Grades before Agreement** setting affects the assessment process only if **Assessments must be agreed** is set to **Yes**. If **Hide Grades before Agreement** is set to **Yes**, the numeric parts of a project's evaluation are hidden from other reviewers. The reviewers can see each other's comments, but not the grades they've assigned. The grades will appear after the reviewers have chosen the same grade, or the closing time has passed.

Maximum Size sets the size limit for project files uploaded to the workshop. This cannot be greater than the limit set for the site.

Schedule for submitting the work and assessments

The fields for **Start and End of Submissions/Assessments** determine when the workshop opens and closes. On the closing date, students can no longer upload files or evaluate others' work. If any grades are hidden, they appear.

You can start the assessments before the end of the submissions. This will give students more time to assess their classmates' work. You can also have a delay between the end of submissions and the beginning of assessments. This gives you time to examine the submissions before having the class assess them. You can determine whether the work is close to what you expected or were trying to elicit from the students. You might even want to use the time between submission and assessment to refine your assessment criteria, in response to the work submitted.

Summary

The key to a Workshop is not what kind of work you will have the students submit, but your assessment strategy. An assessment strategy determines what the students assess, how they assess, whether they must agree on their assessments, whether their assessments must agree with yours, and how much of their grade depends upon completing assessments.

As you set up the Workshop, be sure to think about how you will tie everything back to learning objectives and how your assessments should be measurable. They should also indicate to the student where there may be gaps in skills or knowledge. In participating in the required tasks in the workshop, students will learn from each other as they collaborate and then assess each other's work.

If the work that the student produces is the most important part, you may as well use a simple Assignment instead. It is the assessment strategy that makes a workshop different from the other modules.

11
Portfolio/Gallery Solution

As you were putting together your workshop solution, you probably noticed that it has the perfect structure for showcasing and evaluating projects and other capstone-type student activities. Not only does it allow students to post and share their work and comment in an ongoing way, but it also allows them to modify their displayed work and even put together joint projects.

Now you can build a workshop, but, instead of simply using it as a place to collaborate, you're using it as a place to display and showcase a body of work. How? The answer is really quite simple. It's in the palm of your hands.

Keep in mind that the biggest hurdle has already been overcome. You've already learned how to put together workshops and you know how to implement strategies for encouraging students to contribute their work and ideas. Keep in mind that the workshop format is ideal for encouraging students to pursue their own interests and to choose topics that are relevant to them.

Because of the interaction with fellow students and also the ability to work on topics that are interesting, which results in a sense of accomplishment, the workshop format is highly motivating.

That said, it makes perfect sense to use the workshop format for other purposes, to take advantage of Moodle's flexibility and interactivity-grounded philosophy of instructional design.

This chapter will cover ways to customize the workshop activity/format and use it for collaborative student activities that tie in well with the course you're designing. As you read this chapter, keep a good idea of what you'd like to accomplish in your course (the course outcomes) and think about which of the options that we cover could be ideal for your purposes.

Now that you've learned how to put together the workshop activity, let's explore all the things we can do with it. Student presentations, creative writing projects, student digital art, mashups, videos, portfolios, and research projects are just some of the possibilities.

Learning objectives and outcomes

Creating a gallery or portfolio of student work gives you an opportunity to constantly refer back to your learning objectives and outcomes. It's a great way to incorporate more than one learning objective or course objective because students will be contributing and assessing more than one piece of work.

It is a good idea to refer back to learning objectives as you create rubrics and also provide a framework for feedback.

Advantages of collaborative activities

Collaborative activities inspire learners to connect with each other and they help build confidence. People learn from each other and so they have a space to share ideas to build upon what they've seen in the collaboration space (the workshop) and in their previous experiences.

Being able to draw on prior knowledge is very important to adult learners and so the portfolio or gallery is particularly useful in courses for professional development, licensing, or career advancement.

Project-based assessment

Think about the ways that you assessed student work, as well as student participation in the workshops that you built in the last chapter. Do you remember how you assigned a grade for the way that students assessed each other? It may not have seemed like a very important detail at that time, but what you were doing was, in reality, fundamental to the successful operation of a portfolio or gallery type of assignment.

In assessing student performance in a project, keep in mind that you are assessing much more than the final project that has been submitted. You are assessing the way students demonstrate whether they achieved learning objectives that include collaboration, creative problem-solving, synthesis, and application of knowledge. If you are familiar with Bloom's taxonomy, you'll recognize right away that they are in the higher-level cognitive skills in

Bloom's taxonomy.

The best uses of project-based assessment

Project-based assessment is most effective when it is used on the last assignment of the course and when it reflects the culmination of a full term of study. For that reason, it can be a portfolio or gallery assignment and you can use it as a capstone project.

Students generally respond quite well to portfolio or gallery projects because they enjoy being able to see what other students are doing. In addition, they're able to break the work down into stages, which allays pressure and gives them an opportunity to see what others are doing and thinking. Because you're giving the students the opportunity to add, comment, edit, and revise the work after it's in the gallery or portfolio, you're encouraging them to put to use the ideas that they have after viewing their peers' work. In doing so, you're motivating your students and, at the same time, you're helping them develop meta-cognitive skills.

Ideally, the project brings together all the topics of the course and allows students to perform their own research and add their own ideas. Projects can be done with the students working together in teams or partnerships or they can work alone.

Learning objectives and projects

Before you ask students to pull together all their work in the course so far in order to create a portfolio to share with the class, or to bring together information to make a final presentation; make sure that the work will be aligned with the overall course outcomes.

Portfolios are fun, but they need to be sure to satisfy a real purpose and help students demonstrate that they've achieved the learning goals.

Typically, learning objects that require students to analyze a case study, pull together an exhibit of examples, present findings from a research project, or demonstrate the results of mapping or lab work, can be well served through the portfolio/gallery process.

Collaboration and cooperation

While it is not necessary for students to collaborate in the assembling of materials for their gallery or portfolio, collaboration and cooperation are necessary, at least in the open presentation phase.

After the materials have been posted, students have the opportunity to comment and grade their fellow students' work. They may even choose to post their response within the individual portfolio. How might it work? What would a response look like? Think of a discussion board. You can have discussion responses and encourage students to post their thoughts—either as text or as audio/video commentary.

Also, think of social networking and the way that people respond. The portfolio integrates the energy of YouTube and Facebook. How? Think of the *reaction videos* that people often post. One reaction will trigger another reaction and so on-before you know it, you've watched a dozen or so reactions. You're right in the middle of a *conversation* and what Mikhael Bakhtin called the *dialogical imagination*.

Examples of portfolios and galleries

This is not an exhaustive list. These are just a few ideas to help you get started. After we list examples, we'll post sample/example assignments for a Portfolio assignment. Entitled My Hometown, the assignment is a point of departure and designed to help you get started and to spur your own ideas and innovative thinking. You will have students review each others work. That will assure collaboration and also allow students to learn from each other. The instructor will also assess the work.

Multimedia presentations

Students have an opportunity to post a wide array of files in their projects. For example, let's consider a gallery that has to do with examples of the importance of Plato's philosophy in today's world.

Let's start by adding a new workshop and titling it **Plato in Today's World**:

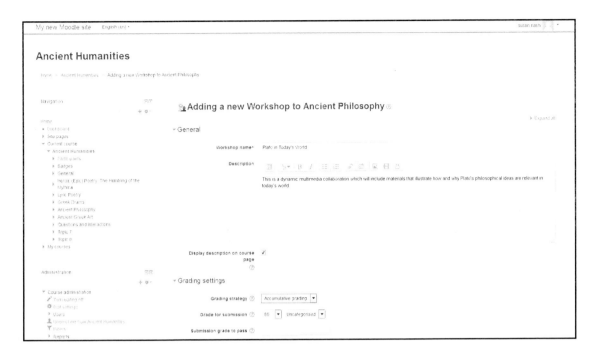

Now, let's define the themes to be represented in the portfolio or gallery. Remember, students can submit presentations, movies, images, sound files, documents, and more.

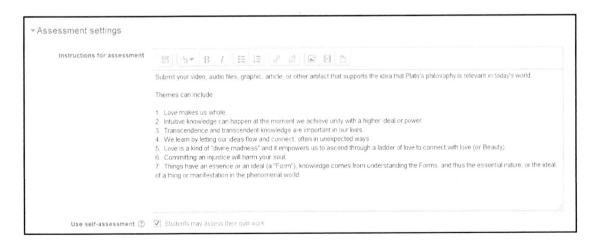

If a student submits an image or a video, it is a good idea to ask them to accompany the file with an explanation.

Otherwise, the connections to the topic and the outcomes may not be clear. For example, let's take a look at Paul Klee's painting-*Static-Dynamic Intensification*.

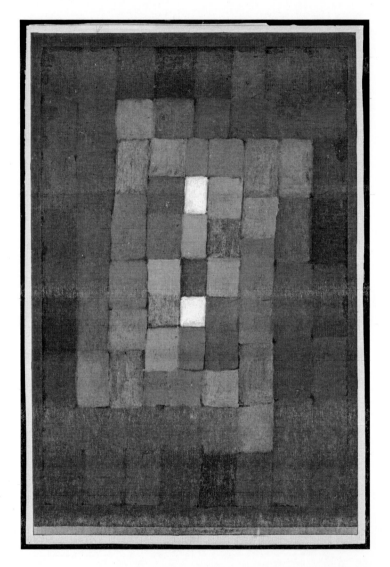

Without an explanation of how it can represent Plato's notion of ascending intellectually to a point of transcendence in which illuminations and new knowledge gained via inductive reasoning are acquired, then the image does not quite connect to the course topic.

Student presentations

Students can post presentations on topics they've researched earlier in the course. The presentations can use presentation software, as well as text, video, audio, and images (diagrams, maps, graphics, and so on).

Student image galleries

If your course involves art appreciation, film appreciation, art history, or other highly visual topics, you may ask students to post images.

Also, students can post images from field work. They can post images from outcrops or fossils collected on a field trip for a geology course.

Alternatively, if it is a design course (graphics, web design, and so on), the image gallery is a perfect place for students to share their work.

Student creative writing projects

While the portfolio is outstanding for bringing together a set of journals and student writings, there is no reason to restrict oneself to writing.

Encourage students to post photos, images, maps, satellite images, mashups, and other elements that reinforce the creative flow of thoughts, ideas, and emotions.

Student research projects

Students can share their research papers and any original research they may have done in conjunction with their research project. For example, they can post their papers and their annotated bibliography. At the same time, they can include laboratory measurements, data collected from the field, or interviews. If they include results from questionnaires, they can also post their research design and the rationale for their research design/process.

Encouraging creativity – A sample workshop

Portfolio and gallery assignments, if well-designed with positive feedback from the instructor, can encourage student creativity.

The creative writing e-portfolio – My Hometown

Memoirs and autobiographical reflections are an excellent way to engage students in a creative writing project and are something that they can easily share.

Instructions to students

You will upload and post the following documents and files in your e-portfolio:

- **Early memory**: What are your earliest recollections of your hometown? Please post a 500-word reflection of an early memory of your hometown. Be sure to incorporate several events and open with an illustrative scene. As you write, be sure to incorporate vivid descriptions and details.

- **Edgy memory**: What memories make you uncomfortable? Why? Explore the issues that surface as you write about something that makes you feel a bit on edge. Be sure to incorporate descriptions of the key people. In addition, do not forget to discuss the contexts, histories, demographics, and political/environmental issues that might provide insight into your emotional discomfort. Do not feel compelled to share information that is too personal and, by the same token, feel free to fictionalize your memoir. The word count for this writing should be at least 1000 words.

- **Music and words**: Does a particular song reflect your thoughts? If so, link to it (if you can find it on YouTube or another free site). Also, record your thoughts on the voiceboard. You may use Audacity (open source software available from SourceForge) and upload to a location on the web that you can then link to. Write a reflective essay of at least 250 words. Include two or three flash memories.

- **Images**: Video or photos. Do you have images that help express your emotions? Or, do you have images of you hometown? If so, please link to them or upload them here. If you have a video you'd like to share, you may upload to YouTube and then embed the html code here or, alternatively, post a link.

- **Recent memories or thoughts about your hometown**: Write a 750-word meditation of what your hometown means to you. It does not have to be a narrative with a certain theme or purpose. It can be a mosaic of "flash memories" or a kind of collage of random thoughts interspersed with statistics, billboard text, snippets from the local radio, overheard conversation, physical descriptions of the people, places, and events, along with your personal thoughts about the meaning(s) (or lack of) of the idea of roots and a place-based identity.

Procedures for collaboration

As the instructor, you'll have many opportunities to encourage responses from your students. Set up a discussion forum. As in the workshop example, you can require students to *grade* each other.

As you encourage students to grade each other, keep in mind that they are being graded for participation and encouraging creativity, not shutting down the creative process.

At the same time, encourage students to post responses to the different posts. The responses can take the form of *conversations* and can refer directly to another student's work. Make sure that the students are respectful of each other's' works and that they do not create parodies or satires of them. While it's permissible to parody the classics and major political/cultural figures, it is most decidedly not acceptable for students to satirize each others work. If they do, it is usually perceived as mocking and could be considered a form of harassment. So, be sure to set very clear ground rules.

Our hometowns – A collective conversation

The final step in this assignment takes place after students have posted their own e-portfolio material and then have responded to each other's work by posting comments, responding to discussion threads, and posting their own specific responses to individual works.

Encourage students to look at the conversations/responses and to put an asterisks next to their favorite ones. Then, select one from each student to put in the *Collective Conversation*. It will be a collage of written responses. If students respond with recorded conversations, mashups of audio, or video responses, you can select among them and post them too.

What results will be an almost magical patchwork quilt of collective thoughts and human emotion about hometowns and identity. You will be amazed at the kinds of social issues that come to the surface and the themes that emerge. The quality of the final project/collage is often high enough to be published in an online journal or blog.

Supportive environments and intellectual risk taking

As we saw in the previous section (in the sample assignment, `My Hometown`), it is very important to set ground rules in order to maintain a supportive environment. You can do a great deal to assure students that they are going to be rewarded for their efforts. Pay attention to them. Praise efforts publicly. Post encouraging thoughts and ideas in the discussion board. Make sure that your suggestions are clear and that they directly relate to the students' efforts.

One of the overarching goals and outcomes in any sort of project or portfolio is to foster a positive self-concept and a willingness to take risks-even make missteps and mistakes. Remind your students that they should experiment. After all, that's how we learn. And it's a key to the kind of experiential learning we'd like to foster in the Moodle environment.

A portfolio assignment such as `My Hometown` is a perfect bridge project that brings about both vicarious learning as well as experiential. It refers back to the individual student's memory of his/her hometown and helps them connect emotionally as well as intellectually to a set of ideas and new intellectual configurations—all of which allow them to think in new ways and to reconfigure their own perception.

At the same time, it's very important to let the students know that relating to their own experience is only half of the story.

The other half is reading the experiences of other students and entering into an emotional *conversation* with them, as their own ideas, thoughts, memories, beliefs, and values are triggered, challenged, and brought to the surface.

The final collage (the "Our Hometowns: A Collective Conversation") can be something very rewarding—a source of pride for the participants. While the e-portfolio itself is a showcase, the collective work is a showcase of its own and there is no question that it can inspire everyone, even departments and creative programs in other schools, colleges, and universities.

With Moodle 3.0's enhanced ability to integrate social networking, it's possible to embed RSS feeds and tools such as social bookmarking (del.icio.us, digg, and so on) as well as Facebook and Twitter.

Tips for a successful experience

As you work with your students, there are a number of ways you can guide them and help them successfully complete the tasks and achieve the learning objectives.

- **Set a positive tone**: This is how you can get your students to submit their work.
- **Encourage connections to real-life interests**: As we could see in the case of the *My Hometown* activity, students are motivated when they can see connections to their lives, their interests, beliefs, and values. The more you encourage connections to real-life interests, the more "real" the assignment will feel and the

more "buy-in" you'll get from your students. They will intellectually and emotionally invest in the activity.

- **Provide examples and models**: It is always good to be able to provide examples and models; however, there is a danger in this. If you're too explicit, chances are that you'll end up having a lot of copies of your model, rather than free-thinking ideas and creative self-expression. So, provide some examples, but even more importantly, encourage participation and acknowledge/reward excellent work. Encourage students to experiment and to think freely.
- **Stay involved**: Don't suffocate your students. However, don't fail to encourage them and to guide them as they take risks. Chances are that you'll have to field quite a few technical questions, particularly if your e-portfolios include text, videos, images, and audio files, as well as responses and social networking feeds and sharing. Encourage experiments and out-of-the-box thinking and even consider hybrid solutions that utilize mobile devices along with Moodle's online format.

Summary

One of the most satisfying aspects of an online learning experience is to be able to participate in a capstone experience, or a final project, which allows the student to pull together things they've learned in the class and to connect them to their own experience. It is even more satisfying when the student can see what others are creating and then flow with it, engaging in a lively, energetic, and inspiring exchange of ideas, experiences, perspectives, and vantage points.

Moodle allows you to do all that and then to bring in the power of social networking, if you so desire. But social networking outside Moodle is not really the point. The key is to create a social network and a learning community in the here and now of your course, which has the potential to inspire and to live on in the hearts and minds of your students.

We've reviewed a number of possible ways to use the workshop experience as a foundation and a point of departure for others. Specifically, we've discussed how you can build a place for students to display and share their work. The e-portfolios and galleries that they participate in allow them to showcase their work, share with others, collaborate and cooperate with fellow students, and finally to create a collective final artifact/project.

As you work with Moodle, you may wish to check out Mahara, which is another open-source platform. Mahara provides an e-portfolio platform, which allows you to share files and collaborate in a very seamless and intuitive way.

Collaboration can be transformative, particularly when it's in a situation where students may have felt isolated before the course or if they've lacked motivation due to missing out on a sense of affiliation. The workshop/gallery/portfolio capability of Moodle allows you that power.

Index